GUN SMUGGLING,
CASTRO'S CUBA
AND THE
PITTSBURGH MAFIA

GUN SMUGGLING, CASTRO'S CUBA

AND THE

PITTSBURGH MAFIA

Richard Gazarik

THE
History
PRESS

Published by The History Press
Charleston, SC
www.historypress.com

First published 2025

Manufactured in the United States

ISBN 9781467157636

Library of Congress Control Number: 2024944902

Notice: The information in this book is true and complete to the best of our knowledge. It is offered without guarantee on the part of the author or The History Press. The author and The History Press disclaim all liability in connection with the use of this book.

To my own mob: Evie, Camryn, Nora and Blake

CONTENTS

ACKNOWLEDGEMENTS

New Kensington, Pennsylvania, has always been a rough, gritty city founded on hard work. The city and surrounding towns produced coal, steel, glass, aluminum and the "rackets." The 1940s through the 1960s was considered the golden age of Mafia rule. New Ken, as locals referred to their hometown, was populated with bookie joints, gambling casinos, horse parlors, slot machines, after-hours clubs and brothels from the 1940s through the early 1970s. I grew up in the Alle-Kiski Valley and knew the characters in this book by reputation. Everyone knew the Mafia existed. Everybody knew a bookie. Everybody knew where to play a number, hoping to score some extra cash on the 600 to 1 payoff. The Mafia thrived if New Kensington thrived because Alcoa was the biggest employer, with several thousand workers who were a major source of gambling revenue. To better understand this era, I recommend reading Jeanine Mazak-Kahne's doctoral dissertation "Small-Town Mafia: Organized Crime in New Kensington, Pennsylvania," which details the economic relationship between the Mafia and Alcoa. Carl Meyerhuber's article "Organizing Alcoa: The Aluminum Workers Union in Pennsylvania's Allegheny Valley, 1900–1971," explains the creation of the union movement. Two other works by Meyerhuber, "Black Valley: Pennsylvania's Alle-Kisi Valley and the Great Strike of 1919" and "The Alle-Kiski Coal Wars, 1913–1919," were also insightful. Finally, Quentin Skrabec, in his book, *Aluminum in America: A History*, is also worth reading. This is my seventh book. My editors J. Banks Smither and Abigail Fleming helped guide this book through the home stretch. Special thanks also go to retired journalist Paul Hess for his time and recollections about his years writing about the Mafia and city of New Kensington, Pennsylvania.

PREFACE

This book is a history about a branch of the Pittsburgh Mafia in the New Kensington area, but it is also a history of a city with an industrial heritage that spent decades trying to live down its seedy, violent reputation as "Little Chicago" and as a mecca for gambling because of the control of organized crime local law enforcement and politics. When I was ten years old, the New Kensington Mafia became front-page news when several of its members attempted to fly a shipment of stolen military weapons from a rural airport in neighboring Allegheny County and were nabbed by federal agents in West Virginia when the pilot stopped for fuel. Local newspapers, the *Valley Daily News* and the *New Kensington Daily Dispatch*, led by its crusading editor Gene Simon, wrote about the mob and provided the FBI with information about its illegal activities. Paul Hess was a young reporter in the late 1950s when he was assigned to cover New Kensington. Working out of an office in a former gas station, Hess covered the police and city hall and occasionally rubbed shoulders with mobsters. Hess recalled making the rounds one night in 1962 when one of Mannarino's henchmen, Abe Zeid, was brought into the emergency room at Citizens General Hospital with a gunshot wound to the stomach. "He was laying in the parking lot. Can you imagine that?" recalled Hess. Police initially suspected that Zeid was the target of a gangland hit, but it was later revealed he was shot in Pittsburgh by a tavern owner who owed the Mannarinos a $2,000 gambling debt and decided to shoot it out with Zeid rather than pay, according to FBI reports. Zeid's brother-in-law drove him from Pittsburgh to New Kensington so police wouldn't learn about the shootout.

"I never knew why Gene had such an obsession with the Mafia," Hess told the author. "I do not know. He never said why." Simon refused to let up on the mob. He provided information to FBI agents and spearheaded a movement to clean up the city by backing candidates who refused to make deals with corrupt politicians in hock to the Mafia. FBI special agent Bernard Brown interviewed Simon on July 3, 1961, and Simon told him "he and his newspaper are taking and will continue to take a vigorous role in a growing campaign in New Kensington to rid the town of the reputation of being racket dominated."

A history of New Kensington and the Mafia during the 1950s and 1960s is not documented in history books but is available to the public in declassified CIA and FBI files at the National Archives and Records Administration at College Park, Maryland. I visited the archives in the mid-'90s when the first batch of files were made public while I was working as a reporter on a series of stories about the Mafia titled "Mob Rule." The documents were made public under the President John F. Kennedy Assassination Records Collection Act passed in 1992. Additional records have been released periodically since 2017. Some of the records deal with possible Mafia involvement in Kennedy's murder and mention New Kensington mobsters and their associates who drew the attention of the House Select Committee on Assassinations.

The documents reveal details about events in New Kensington that the public never knew about. "We covered stories we knew about," Hess continued. "We reported on what we could see from the outside. We knew very little about what was going on behind the scenes."

The thousands of pages of documents must be read with a jaundiced eye. After chasing communist spies in the early days of the Cold War, the FBI had to focus on the Mafia after the 1957 mob summit meeting in Apalachin, New York, and scrambled to learn about the mob and relied heavily on informants for their information. In the late 1950s, agents were in the dark about the Mafia and weren't sure what to call the criminal organization. Their reports contain references to the "Outfit," the "Syndicate" and the "Onorata Societa." By 1963, the bureau had whittled the names down to "Our Thing," "La Cosa Nostra," "La Causa Nostra," "A Causa Nostra," according to an August 12, 1963 memo from J. Edgar Hoover to the New York field office.

The records are now online at the archives as well as at the Mary Ferrell Foundation, a nonprofit organization that provides access to thousands of pages of documents related to the assassination of President John Kennedy. Another online repository is the Black Vault, which contains millions of pages of government documents, including records on the Mafia and Kennedy assassination. There are also the records of the Church Committee, which investigated abuses by the CIA and FBI, and the House Select Committee on Assassinations.

The records paint a disturbing portrait of an era in a region where government officials, from Pennsylvania governors and congressmen to small-town mayors, accepted payoffs from mafiosi to protect their criminal enterprises. Richard Thornburgh, then U.S. attorney for western Pennsylvania, coined the phrase "politico-racket complex" to describe the illicit ties between the Mafia and police and elected officials. He said the Mafia had a "near stranglehold" in communities throughout the western part of the state.

By 1972, Thornburgh had amassed over one hundred indictments for gambling, narcotics, public corruption, mail fraud and labor racketeering against mobsters and their associates in western Pennsylvania. Two years later, he exposed a decades-long pattern of corruption among law enforcement that targeted a district attorney, police and public officials. Despite the indictments and continuing investigations, the Mafia remained active until the federal government dismantled the mob in the 1990s through aggressive investigations and successful prosecutions. Prison, old age and death contributed to the mob's demise; the Mafia ran out of leaders, and there were no younger mafiosi to step up and assume the mantle of leadership.

INTRODUCTION

Aluminum made the city of New Kensington, Pennsylvania, famous. The Mafia made it infamous. FBI records detail the history of the once thriving Aluminum City, the birthplace of Alcoa and the aluminum industry.

For decades, members of the Pittsburgh Mafia ruled New Kensington and the surrounding Alle-Kiski Valley, controlling politics, elections and local government while raking in millions of dollars from gambling, extortion, loan sharking and prostitution. They were allowed to operate by corrupt cops and public officials who ignored the mob's criminal enterprises and reaped financial rewards for their averted eyes.

New Kensington is part of the Allegheny-Kiskiminetas River valleys, a collection of industrial towns that includes Arnold, Lower Burrell and Vandergrift in Westmoreland County; Harrison Township, Brackenridge, Tarentum and East Deer in Allegheny County; and Leechburg and Apollo in Armstrong County. The Conemaugh River joins the Loyalhanna to form the Kiskiminetas River, which enters the Allegheny River where it separates the two valleys. The district once was known as the "Black Valley" in the early decades of the twentieth century because of the militant anti-union stance adopted by local corporations, which refused to recognize unions and hired scabs to break strikes in the coal fields and steel mills.

Native Americans first populated the region. English, Scottish, Irish and German immigrants came in the 1700s followed by Slavs, Italians and

Top: Alcoa plant in New Kensington as seen across the Allegheny River. *Library of Congress.*

Bottom: One of the first buildings of Alcoa. *Library of Congress.*

Jews. Glass manufacturing companies imported glassblowers from France and Belgium, and steel companies brought in African Americans from the South along with Greeks and Syrians as strikebreakers, according to a 1993 ethnographic survey of the Alle-Kiski Valley conducted by the Rivers of Steel Heritage Corporation.

John LaRocca, boss of the Pittsburgh Mafia. *Wikipedia*.

The Mafia's roots in the city run deep. John Bazzano, once boss of the Mafia in Pittsburgh, began his criminal career in New Kensington and became a rich man during Prohibition by selling yeast and sugar to bootleggers. He succeeded Pittsburgh boss Giuseppe Siragusa, who ruled the Mafia from 1929 to 1931 until he was murdered. Bazzano's reign was also short. He reigned from 1931 to 1932 and was murdered in New York City on orders by the Mafia's ruling commission for ordering the murders of brothers John, Arthur and James Volpe in Pittsburgh. Bazzano was summoned to New York, where the Mafia's rulers ordered him killed for failing to seek permission for the hit on the Volpes.

The Pittsburgh Mafia was ruled for decades by John LaRocca, who initially controlled the rackets in Allegheny, Blair, Beaver, Butler, Cambria, Fayette, Mercer, Washington and Westmoreland Counties before expanding to include eastern Ohio and northern West Virginia from 1956 until he died in 1984. LaRocca was succeeded by Mike Genovese. LaRocca was among the nation's Mafia bosses who attended the 1957 mob summit in Apalachin, New York, along with Pittsburgh mobsters Frank Amato Sr., Mike Genovese and Frank Valenti when police disrupted a meeting of sixty gangsters at the home of mobster Joseph Barbara, who hosted the meeting.

LaRocca's organization was one of five crime families that controlled Pennsylvania. Angelo Bruno was the boss in Philadelphia until he was murdered. Russell Bufalino oversaw the rackets in the northeastern part of the state until he died in 1994. Sam "Sam the Plumber" DeCavalcante of New Jersey ruled Bucks County, Pennsylvania, while Stefano Magaddino ran Erie County from his base in New York until he died in 1974.

The small, tight-knit LaRocca organization was one of the most disciplined and aggressive clans in the county, according to the FBI, and two of its most

Mob Kingpin Cars at Apalachin, 1957

Above: Limousines of Mafia bosses parked at the estate of Joseph Barbara in Apalachin, New York. *Monmouth County, New York.*

Right: Joseph Barbara hosted the 1957 mob summit. *Wikipedia.*

powerful members were brothers, Samuel and Gabriel "Kelly" Mannarino of New Kensington, who controlled the Alle-Kiski Valley.

The brothers were greedy, violent men. They bribed cops, judges, prosecutors and politicians in exchange for protection. They chose candidates for public office, rigged elections and financed political campaigns through gambling. New Kensington was the fiefdom of the Mannarino brothers, and they silently ruled the city as if they owned it—in a way, they did. Their influence was embedded in the political and social fabric of not only New Kensington but also the entire Alle-Kiski Valley. FBI director J. Edgar Hoover considered the Mannarinos among the top mafiosi in the United States. He made them a target of the bureau's Top Hoodlum Program and ordered his agents in Pittsburgh to pursue them.

1
TAKEOFF

The twin-engine Beechcraft revved its engines and slowly taxied onto the grass airstrip at a rural airport near Tarentum, Pennsylvania, before lumbering down the 1,800-foot runway at the Allegheny Valley Airport, twelve miles northeast of Pittsburgh, on November 4, 1958. The plane's tail wheel was nearly flat from the weight of the 1,200-pound cargo inside the fuselage, which caused the plane's wings to wobble on takeoff. The plane pierced through the ground fog and climbed for six minutes to an altitude of 1,025 feet before the pilot, Stuart Sutor, began hedgehopping to avoid the radar at the Allegheny County Airport thirty miles away in West Mifflin.

Sutor was piloting a Beechcraft 18-D, a large, lumbering aircraft that was outfitted to carry passengers or cargo. He was trying to avoid being tracked on radar because the plane was loaded with stolen military weapons destined for Fidel Castro in Cuba, who was waging guerrilla war against dictator Fulgencio Batista.

When the aircraft landed a short time later in Morgantown, West Virginia, to refuel, Sutor was arrested and the contraband weapons cache was

Pilot Stuart Sutor was arrested when he landed in West Virginia with a load of military weapons stolen from a National Guard Armory in Ohio. *Wikipedia.*

Twin-engine Beechcraft similar to the aircraft used by gun smugglers trying to ship guns to Fidel Castro. *National Air and Space Museum.*

seized by federal agents, triggering an international investigation stretching from Ohio to Pennsylvania, Chicago, New York, Florida, Canada, Switzerland, Lichtenstein, Italy and Cuba. Six men, all with ties to the Mafia in New Kensington, were arrested, but that wasn't the end the story. It was just the beginning.

The gunrunning operation is detailed in declassified FBI files contained in a 1977 report issued by the House Select Committee on Assassinations, which reinvestigated the 1963 Kennedy assassination. During the congressional probe, the names of Sam and Kelly Mannarino surfaced as committee investigators examined whether any members of the Mafia, including members of the LaRocca clan, were involved in Kennedy's murder because of the Mannarinos' links to gambling in Havana and their ties to mobster Norman "Roughhouse" Rothman. Rothman fronted a casino for the brothers in Cuba and was a close associate of Tampa mob boss Santo Trafficante Jr., whom government investigators suspected may have been involved in Kennedy's murder along with Louisiana mobster Carlos Marcello and Teamsters president Jimmy Hoffa.

Did the Mafia kill Kennedy? Was there a government coverup? Was the CIA involved? Investigators ruled out Soviet, Cuban and anti-Castro exile involvement in the assassination, but there is circumstantial—not direct—evidence linking the CIA to the killing. The committee concluded, "La Cosa Nostra had a strong motive for taking drastic action. Yet it is extremely unlikely that it would have considered such a major and dangerous act as assassinating the president…but the evidence does not preclude the possibility individual members may have been involved." The committee's chief counsel, G. Robert Blakey, was more candid, telling the *New York Times* in 1979, "I think the mob did it."

The House Select Committee's probe discredited the Warren Commission investigation, which concluded that Lee Harvey Oswald was the lone gunman and discounted any evidence of a conspiracy. The Warren Commission failed to question important witnesses, and the FBI and the CIA withheld evidence. The Commission concluded that Oswald shot the president from a sixth-story window of the Texas School Book Depository as he traveled through Dallas on November 22, 1963. After shooting Kennedy, Oswald killed Dallas police officer J.D. Tippit, and Oswald was subsequently killed by Dallas strip club owner Jack Ruby, who had ties to the Mafia and may have been involved in gunrunning.

The Church Committee, named after Idaho senator Frank Church, was formed in 1975 to investigate the assassination of foreign leaders by the CIA and abuses by the FBI. It conducted a limited probe into the Kennedy assassination. The Church Committee's formal name was the Committee to Study Governmental Operations with Respect to Intelligence Activities and reviewed CIA attempts to kill Castro and the use of the Mafia to carry

A Mafia canary "sings" before congressional hearing detailing the hierarchy of the Mafia and its leaders. *Library of Congress.*

out the assassination. The House Select Committee did a deeper dive into the assassination, and its investigators concluded that Lee Harvey Oswald and a second gunman killed Kennedy, but they were unable to identify the second triggerman.

The House Committee examined the possibility that Sam Mannarino and Norman Rothman were involved because of allegations that Tampa Mafia boss Santo Trafficante Jr. told anti-Castro activist and exile José Alemán that Kennedy would not be reelected president "because he was going to be hit." Committee investigators wanted to know whether Aleman ever heard Mannarino and Rothman use the same phrase in his presence. Aleman was the son of José Braulio Alemán, Cuba's minister of education under President Ramón Grau San Martín.

The committee knew Louisiana crime boss Carlos Marcello of New Orleans hated Attorney General Robert F. Kennedy, who had deported Marcello to Guatemala. Marcello was born in the North African county of Morocco but claimed he was a citizen of Guatemala and produced a bogus Guatemalan birth certificate, which led Kennedy to deport Marcello as an undesirable alien.

In its final report, the House Select Committee believed Marcello, Trafficante and Hoffa "had the motive, means and opportunity" to assassinate the president, wrote attorney Ronald Goldfarb in the *Washington Post* in 1993. Goldfarb worked for Robert Kennedy in the Organized Crime Division at the Department of Justice.

The Mannarinos had an interest in gambling in the mob's Havana playground in the 1950s thanks to their friendship with dictator Fulgencio Batista, who permitted the brothers to place two thousand slot machines throughout the island and run the gambling concession at the Sans Souci, a nightclub and casino located on the outskirts of Havana. The Mafia had landed in Cuba, building hotels and operating high-end casinos and nightclubs, raking in millions of dollars, but the Mannarinos were small fry compared to their fellow mobsters like Trafficante and Meyer Lansky, a Jewish gangster considered the mastermind of the Mafia's Cuban gambling empire.

While the Mafia enriched themselves, it failed to see trouble on the horizon in the form of a young, bearded, cigar-smoking revolutionary named Fidel Castro who was threatening to upend Batista's cozy relationship with the Mafia by waging guerrilla warfare against his regime. Castro launched his revolution from the hot, steamy jungle and the Sierra Maestra Mountains, killing and bombing his way to Havana.

Left: Gabriel "Kelly" Mannarino was a Pittsburgh area mafiosi who attended the infamous 1957 mob summit in Apalachin, New York. *Wikipedia.*

Right: Sam Mannarino, along with his brother Gabriel "Kelly" Mannarino, controlled New Kensington and surrounding areas in the Alle-Kiski Valley for decades. Both were captains in the Mafia family led by John LaRocca of Pittsburgh. *Wikipedia.*

Castro was cast as a mythic figure by journalists, mainly by *New York Times* reporter Herbert Matthews, who portrayed him as an iconic, romantic revolutionary. Castro was thought to be dead, but Matthews's interview at Castro's mountain base on February 17, 1957, proved he was very much alive and was considered a journalistic coup at the time. Matthews's articles portrayed Castro's ragtag army as a force to be reckoned with at a time when Castro's rebels were at their weakest point in their revolutionary struggle and in need of weapons. Matthews was openly sympathetic toward Castro and told his readers that Castro was no communist and wanted to free Cuba from Batista's corrupt, ruthless rule. After taking power, Castro presented Matthews with a medal for conducting the interview, but the journalist's work was discredited after Castro embraced communism.

Castro attacked army garrisons and organized an underground resistance network across the island. Batista responded with measures that were so brutal that the United States instituted an arms embargo while the CIA began secretly funneling money to Castro and openly disregarding gun smuggling by Castro supporters from Florida. Rebels sabotaged rail lines. They disrupted communications. They stole arms from the military and assassinated government officials. Eventually, Batista was forced to flee, and Havana surrendered to Castro on January 1, 1959.

Entrance to Sans Souci nightclub. *Wikipedia.*

Sam Mannarino watched the revolution spread across Cuba and envisioned himself as the new gambling czar in a Castro-led government if he could help arm Castro's forces. Norman Rothman advised Mannarino to place his bets on Castro, predicting Castro would continue to allow the casinos to remain in operation under Mafia control after he ousted Batista and would be grateful to those who helped him. Mannarino decided to arm Castro and put into motion a plan to supply him with weapons. But Mannarino, Rothman and the CIA misread Castro's true intentions.

Mannarino told an FBI agent during a casual conversation that he expected to be in the "driver's seat" when Castro assumed power. During a meeting at his New Kensington home on March 14, 1958, Mannarino mentioned to his guests that he was going to Havana for three weeks to study the pineapple industry with the intent of investing, but the true purpose of his visit was to meet with Rothman and formulate a plan to obtain guns, according to FBI records.

What Mannarino failed to understand was that Castro loathed the Mafia as much as Spain and the United States for what they had done to Cuba by profiting from the island's natural resources and turning the island into the "brothel of the Caribbean."

The Mannarinos were never major players in the gaming industry in Cuba. Their operation at the Sans Souci lost money, so they sold their interest to Trafficante in a deal reportedly brokered by Lansky.

Life magazine published an article in its March 10, 1958 edition that reported Batista funneled money mobsters paid him for gambling concessions to his wife's charities, when the money went into Batista's pockets. The article also warned how Castro's guerrilla war against the Batista government could mean that Batista's days as Cuba's leader were numbered. Castro's boldness shook Batista after Castro's forces kidnapped an Argentine race car driver who was supposed to drive in Havana's Gran Premio auto race. Then his rebels robbed the National Bank in Havana, burned a sugar warehouse, wrecked a railroad station, raided a passenger train, blew up a military vehicle and hanged a father and son who were government informers.

Still, Mannarino could not be persuaded to stay out of Cuba's internal politics and went ahead with plans to supply Castro with guns. The plan sounded simple but turned out to be more complex. The plan was supposed to work this way. Guns were stolen from a National Guard armory in Ohio, shipped to New Kensington and then flown to Cuba. The scheme would be financed from the proceeds of a bank heist in Canada of millions of dollars in negotiable securities, which would be used as collateral for loans in Switzerland to buy more guns.

2

WELCOME TO ALUMINUM CITY

Nick Miller was a bookie from Wheeling, West Virginia, who was summoned to a meeting at the home of Sam Mannarino in New Kensington, Pennsylvania, on August 17, 1957. Miller was ushered into the basement, where his brother, Kelly, was waiting along with Johnny Fontana and Abe Zeid. Fontana and Zeid grabbed Miller and held him down in a chair while Sam and Kelly strangled Miller with his necktie. His body was stuffed into the trunk of his blue and white Lincoln, driven to the Pittsburgh suburb of Wilkinsburg and left parked on a street for six days until the putrid stench of his decomposing body and a swarm of flies buzzing around the vehicle attracted a passing mailman, who called the police.

"There must have been at least a thousand flies all over the windshield," said mailman Robert Frederick to the *Wheeling Intelligencer*. There also was a terrible odor. "I knew something was dead."

Police popped the trunk and found Miller's body clad in underpants and socks. The remains were so badly decayed that the coroner was unable to determine the cause of death. Miller's brother identified his body by a tattoo of 1930s cartoon character Betty Boop on his bicep and a gold capped tooth, according to the *Pittsburgh Post-Gazette*. Detectives also found a gray sports coat with Miller's initials stitched on an inside pocket.

The thin, balding forty-five-year-old Nick Miller, whose real name was Vosvick, was an ex-con with thirty-seven gambling rests. He operated the Pirate Inn, a Wheeling gambling joint, and began his criminal career working for Wheeling racketeer Big Bill Lias, a 450-pound thug who owned the Wheeling Downs Racetrack until the government seized it and sold it to recoup $3 million in taxes that Lias owed the government, according to the *New York Times*.

Lias was the lord of gambling, prostitution and murder in Wheeling and had ties with the infamous Purple Gang in Detroit. The track was purchased from the United States by the Hazel Park Racing Association in Hazel Park, Michigan, which was managed by Detroit mobsters Tony Zerilli and Jack Tocco, who were cousins and considered Mafia royalty because their fathers also were leading Detroit mafiosi. West Virginia law prevented officials with criminal records from holding corporate office, so Zerilli and Tocco were named as advisors and Zerilli later bought out the other stockholders to assume control of Wheeling Downs.

Miller had run afoul of Zerilli and Tocco because he refused to stop taking bets on races at Wheeling Downs, siphoning between $25,000 and $30,000 a day from on-track betting. The new owners were angry and asked the Mannarinos to kill Miller. The brothers were happy to oblige. "The only reason given for the killing of Miller was that the 'outfit' in Detroit, Michigan had requested" it, reported the FBI in 1961.

Aluminum City was the birthplace of Alcoa, but it also was referred to as "Little Chicago" by FBI agents because it was a wide-open town filled with vice where the Mafia was tolerated because elected officials and the police were in cahoots

Big Bill Lias, the crime boss Wheeling and associate of Nick Miller who was murdered by the Mannarinos at the behest of Detroit mobsters. He weighed nearly four hundred pounds and owned the Wheeling Downs Racetrack until it was seized by the government and sold to recoup back taxes. *Ohio County Public Library*.

with racketeers. "Everybody loved the mob. That's the truth," said Paul Hess, a retired executive editor at the former *Valley News Dispatch* in Tarentum, who covered New Kensington as a newly minted reporter in the late 1950s. "It wasn't a center of evil. The average person in New Kensington accepted what was going on. Everybody in town knew about the Mafia. It wasn't a fright to anybody. I know that's hard to believe," he told the author.

New Kensington was one of several mob-controlled towns in southwestern Pennsylvania, such as Wilkinsburg, McKees Rocks, Wilmerding, Turtle Creek, Braddock, Homestead, Pittsburgh, Monessen, Johnstown, Erie and Altoona. "For too many years in too many jurisdictions, public officials and citizens alike have denied the severity of the problem," reported the Pennsylvania Crime Commission in its 1980 study "A Decade of Organized Crime: A Report on Organized Crime." "Syndicated gambling and corruption were accepted as unpleasant but not overly important realities. Apathy toward the effects of syndicated gambling develops a tradition of poor government."

Alcoa's story began with a young chemist from Ohio, Charles Martin Hall, who developed a less expensive method of producing aluminum in 1886 by using a process known as electrolysis. Before that, smelting aluminum was an expensive and time-consuming operation until Hall and French chemist Paul Héroult simultaneously developed the method known as the Hall-Héroult process and shared the patent.

Aluminum is produced by mixing bauxite and aluminum oxide and then treating it with alkali to remove impurities. The aluminum oxide is dissolved in cryolite, which is composed of sodium, aluminum and fluorine. The mixture creates a liquid. An electric current is passed through the solution, which creates aluminum deposits that can then be cast into ingots.

Martin sought help from metallurgist Alfred Hunt, the owner of the Pittsburgh Testing Laboratory, who persuaded a group of investors to finance research and formed the Pittsburgh Reduction Company in Pittsburgh's Strip District on August 8, 1888. Andrew Mellon, who later became President Herbert Hoover's secretary of the treasury, loaned the fledgling company $25,000 to expand, and the company began producing fifty pounds of aluminum a day. By the 1890s, the Pittsburgh Reduction Company had expanded and was producing one thousand pounds a day. Mellon and his brother Richard Beatty Mellon enticed the company to relocate to New Kensington by offering cheap land and coal and no taxes. Pittsburgh Reduction Company became Alcoa in 1907 and built a 173,000-square-foot plant and hired 276 workers. By the 1920s, Alcoa was producing aluminum sheets for automobile bodies, cooking utensils, washing machines, radio parts, airplanes and car radiators.

The city of New Kensington began to take shape in 1890 when the Mellon-owned Burrell Improvement Company purchased land along the east bank of the Allegheny River and began building a town named Kensington after a section of London. There was a Kensington neighborhood in Philadelphia, so the post office added "New" to the city's name to reduce confusion over mail delivery.

The local Board of Trade referred to New Kensington as the "Queen City of Westmoreland County" and the "Metropolis of the Allegheny Valley," according to the *Pittsburgh Gazette Times*. The company sold parcels the following year, and five hundred homes were built. A business district developed. Trolley service started. A railroad station opened. In 1911, the *Pittsburgh Press* in 1911 referred to the city as a "restful little town" with plenty of available jobs.

In addition to Alcoa, other manufacturers that produced steel, stoves, glass, pianos and organs moved into the city. By 1922, there were fifty-seven industrial plants in New Kensington that employed 5,700 and generated an annual payroll of more than $15 million, according to a doctoral dissertation, "Birthplace of Aluminum, Cradle of Crime: Sphere of Influence in the Deindustrialization of New Kensington, Pennsylvania," by Dr. Jeanne Mazak-Kahne. A new municipal building was constructed. Banks opened along with eighteen churches to accommodate the different faiths in addition to bakeries, hotels and variety, clothing, drug, dry goods and hardware stores.

New Kensington was also at the center of the fledgling labor movement. Surrounding mining villages were the scene of coal strikes between 1919

A sign overlooking the Allegheny River that greeted visitors to New Kensington. *Peoples Library*.

and the 1930s as miners fought to form a union and the Communist Party ran candidates for public office during the Great Depression. Fannie Sellins, an organizer for the United Mine Workers of America based in New Kensington, was shot to death in 1919 by deputy sheriffs during a strike in neighboring Allegheny County, making Sellins one of the first martyrs of the labor movement.

References to the city's ties to the aluminum industry were everywhere. A large sign overlooking the Allegheny River proclaimed, "Welcome to the Aluminum City." There was Aluminum City Terrace, a housing development for Alcoa workers built during World War II that was designed by architects Walter Gropius and Marcel Breuer. Alcoa also manufactured Wear-Ever Cookware, which could be found in kitchens across America. The aluminum maker produced a variety of products that remain in use today: tea kettles, pull tab rings for cans, aluminum foil and beer barrels. It also produced aluminum for the engine block for the Wright brothers' aircraft and the lunar landing module for Apollo 11, which landed on the

Left: This booklet displays the products made by Wear-Ever, a subsidiary of Alcoa. *Wikipedia*.

Right: Wear-Ever Catalogue. Alcoa was plagued by theft of Wear-Ever kitchen utensils from its New Kensington warehouse. The FBI suspected some of the dinnerware found its way to a mob-run restaurant in Florida. *Wikipedia*.

The Wear-Ever Building in New Kensington. Wear-Ever Aluminum Co. was a subsidiary of Alcoa until 1982 when it was sold. *Wikipedia*.

moon. The company also maintained the Alcoa Aluminum Club, and Alcoa had a national presence on network television. NBC broadcast the *Alcoa Hour* from 1955 to 1957 and *Alcoa Theater* from 1957 to 1960. ABC ran *Alcoa Premiere* from 1961 to 1963.

Not everything about Aluminum City was related to the product. The Aluminum City Club was a notorious gambling haunt that was operated by the Mannarinos and fronted by a brash loudmouth racketeer named Frank "Frinkie" Phillips. Aluminum City was filled with nightclubs and after-hours joints frequented by off-duty cops, underworld figures and gamblers.

The center of the Mannarinos gambling empire was a plush casino hidden in the basement of the Giuseppe Garibaldi Club, which was founded in 1920, according to real estate records at the Westmoreland County Recorder of Deeds in Greensburg. The club was named after Giuseppe Garibaldi, the Italian general who waged a military campaign to unite the city-states of Italy. The Garibaldi was a social club open to members of Italian descent, but it was the activities going on in the basement of the club that attracted the interest of federal agents.

New Kensington was corrupt to its core. Elections were tainted by fraud. The First Ward, Second District of New Kensington was the city's red-light district, housing three brothels, and was a voting precinct where the dead rose from their graves on Election Day to cast their ballots. The ward was under the political control of Phillips. Mayor Ray Gardlock refused to allow police to crack down on prostitution because he received seventy-five dollars a week for protection from brothel operators.

Hess remembered Phillips as an arrogant bully. "He thought he was a big deal," Hess told the author. Phillips boasted that the police were afraid to touch him. He once entered the police station to brazenly free a prisoner who was his friend without being stopped by police officers. A federal grand jury investigating vote fraud in Westmoreland County uncovered evidence of votes being cast by unregistered voters in a scam orchestrated by Phillips who eventually pleaded guilty to vote fraud and was sentenced to three years in prison.

An FBI agent testified at Phillips's trial that he found that one hundred signatures were forged, and witnesses testified that they saw Phillips stuffing ballot boxes after the polls had closed and dictating names to poll watchers of unregistered individuals to be recorded as voting, according to the *Pittsburgh Sun-Telegraph.* A soldier from New Kensington who was stationed in Europe was certified as voting. Another man was paralyzed and confined to bed but was somehow managed to vote. Another voter was in South America on Election Day but was listed as casting a ballot. Even mobster Kelly Mannarino was listed as voting, although he admitted at Phillips's trial that he didn't vote in the election. Some residents voted twice, once in the morning and again in the evening, according to the *Pittsburgh Post-Gazette.*

The rise of organized crime in cities across America caused concern among the nation's business community. In 1949, the American Municipal Association feared that the Mafia was infiltrating legitimate businesses as fronts for their illicit enterprises and asked the government for help to rid cities of this criminal plague.

Senator Estes Kefauver responded by chairing a senate committee investigating interstate crime and holding hearing focusing on gambling. Attorney General Robert F. Kennedy put New Kensington on the map when he announced his war on crime that led the FBI and IRS to focus on the Mannarinos and LaRocca. In 1963, mob canary Joe Valachi introduced the term "Cosa Nostra" into the American lexicon by naming the Mafia bosses in American cities, including Pittsburgh. John LaRocca was so perplexed by the exposure that he ordered his associates never to mention Valachi's name in his presence. "Joe Valachi never did a decent thing in his life," fumed LaRocca according to a transcript of a wiretap placed by the FBI on one of LaRocca's businesses.

3

THE BROTHERS

Giacinto and Domenica Rugiero were among the more than 600,000 Italians who answered the call of L'America at the turn of the twentieth century. They were born in Amatea, Italy, and immigrated to America, where there was work. Labor recruiters enticed immigrants to leave their homelands to work in the mills, mines and foundries where manpower was needed, especially in the heavily industrial area of southwestern Pennsylvania. Enclaves of Italian immigrants sprouted in places like New Kensington and Arnold in Westmoreland County and in the Bloomfield neighborhood of Pittsburgh and McKees Rocks, located across the Ohio River from Pittsburgh in Allegheny County.

The Rugieros arrived in the United States from Naples in 1897 and settled in Pittsburgh before moving to New Kensington, where they operated a small neighborhood grocery and made moonshine on the side. Giacinto and his son Sam were arrested for operating a still behind their home, and Sam spent time in the federal prison in Atlanta for impersonating a Prohibition agent and extorting money from bootleggers.

In 1925, the family legally changed their name to Mannarino, according to a legal notice in the *Pittsburgh Post* on February 26. The FBI never learned the reason for the name change, but the Mannarinos raised three sons, two of whom would become among the top Mafia hoodlums in the United States and a third who was a drunk and gambler. Salvatore "Sam" Mannarino was born in 1905, followed by Joseph "Jo Jo" Mannarino in 1911 and Gabriel, who went by the nickname Kelly, born in 1915.

Many immigrants of all nationalities made homebrew or wine to satisfy their thirst or to make extra money during Prohibition. William Adams was a competitor of the Mannarinos who operated a still in the basement of his home just three blocks from the Mannarino residence. Adams told Special Agent Richard Gordon Douce in 1958 that during Prohibition a bomb exploded in his home, seriously injuring Adams and killing his sister-in-law. He suspected the Mannarinos planted the bomb, although no one was ever charged.

The Mannarinos were violent people. Their father had "a very mean disposition," carried a gun, a razor and police badge and was investigated in 1958 for threatening to kill a man over a misunderstanding in a bar, according to the FBI. An informant told the FBI in 1937 that Kelly sprayed a two-block area of New Kensington with a machine gun from a passing car but was never arrested. In grade school, he carried a straight razor to threaten other kids, according to a report filed by Special Agent Norman Thompson in February 1958. Domenica Mannarino advised a young Sam to never use a gun unless his back was to the wall and he had no other choice.

Kelly's penchant for violence was illustrated in a 1950 incident at the home of Frank Amato Sr., his father-in-law, who once was the Mafia boss in Pittsburgh. Wilbur Kastle was a small-time hood who forced his way at gunpoint into Amato's Braddock home because he heard rumors that Amato kept $50,000 stashed in a wall safe. While Kastle held the Amato family at bay, an accomplice searched the house for the money. Mannarino, who had been upstairs, came down and shot Kastle three times. The wounded Kastle escaped but was arrested at the hospital.

While he was recovering from his wounds, Amato visited Kastle and told him "he was either insane or didn't know who Amato was," according to a 1958 FBI interview of Kastle in the state penitentiary in Pittsburgh. Amato told Kastle he was a "big man in the Mafia" and offered Kastle a deal. Amato offered him $4,000 and would pay his hospital bills if he kept quiet about Mannarino's involvement in the shooting. If Kastle pleaded guilty to attempted robbery, Amato would put the fix in with the judge so Kastle could be paroled within two years. Kastle was sentenced from five to ten years, and Amato reneged on the deal. "I hope he serves his whole sentence," Amato told an FBI informant.

Sam struck fear in the hearts of Pittsburgh bookies when he and Joe Rosa, another up-and-coming gangster in the Pittsburgh Mafia, used threats of violence to force bookmakers to make them partners in the 1920s and 1930s. "When Jewish gamblers would see Mannarino and Rosa walking down the street together, they all disappeared as though hiding from the plague," reported the FBI in a detailed background report on the family in 1966. He and Rosa would announce to a bookie that they were equal partners in their gambling enterprise, and if they objected, they would pull out their guns, force the gamblers to face the wall and then joked about "how they were going to have their own smaller Pittsburgh versions of the notorious St. Valentine's Day Massacre in Chicago."

Sam and Kelly Mannarino were short, stocky men who never got past the sixth grade. Sam was only five feet, four inches tall. His brother was an inch taller and talked with a lisp and stuttered. FBI reports always noted they should be considered armed and dangerous because they both had quick tempers and were known to carry guns.

Jo Jo was the black sheep of the family—Sam Mannarino told an FBI agent in 1961 that "Jo Jo would bet his last dollar on a race even if he had not had a decent meal in two days." He was banned from New Kensington for writing bad checks that his brothers always made good. The FBI described him in their reports as a "nut" and "con man" whose hands shook with palsy and who stammered when he talked. He married Hazel Stone, the third wife of the late actor Lewis Stone, who played Judge James Hardy, the father of Mickey Rooney's character, Andy Hardy, in a series of movies. Lewis Stone died in 1953 and left his wife an estate valued at $6 million.

Hazel Stone was introduced to FBI agents on April 18, 1958, in Del Mar, California, and told them she "was fully aware of Joseph's weaknesses but that she is content to support him," according to the report by Special Agents John Flanigan and Franklin Wright. Jo Jo Mannarino was interviewed by agents on June 5, 1958, and he described himself as a "gambler, horse player and tout" and "admitted that he is living on his wife's money and spends time doing errands for her when not drinking at some cocktail lounge," according to Pittsburgh-based Special Agent Richard Gordon Douce.

New Kensington's underworld developed in the first decade of the twentieth century when a red-light district opened in the city along with gambling joints to cater to immigrant workers. In the 1920s, the rackets in New Kensington were run by Mike Zervos, a Greek immigrant, who operated a coffee shop as a front for his gambling and morphine dealing business. When Zervos was convicted of murder and sentenced to life in prison, Sam filled the vacuum by organizing the rackets after learning the ropes from Frank Amato and John LaRocca, who was impressed by Sam's ability to "knock heads together," according to a report by Special Agent Thomas Forsyth III in 1961.

Sam surrounded himself with men who had certain skills to build a gambling enterprise. He recruited Willie Sams, a childhood friend who was a top handicapper. He brought in Tom Tannas, who had political connections in Westmoreland County and in the state capital in Harrisburg. He later brought his younger brother, Kelly, into the fold. Sam started his career in the Mafia working as a driver for mob boss John Bazzano, who would become boss of the Mafia in Pittsburgh. He told the FBI he was formally inducted into the Mafia by LaRocca in the 1940s.

Sam married his fifteen-year-old wife, Rose, when he was twenty. She was described in FBI reports as "a quiet, religious woman who is dutiful and obedient to every wish of Sam Mannarino." His first arrest came in 1926 for operating a still. A year later he was charged with impersonating a federal Prohibition agent while extorting money from bootleggers and sentenced to a year in the federal prison in Atlanta, according to the *Gazette Times*.

Sam violated the code of silence among mafiosi known as *omerta*, which required members to pledge to never talk about the organization or to law enforcement. Sam was listed in reports as an FBI informant whether knowingly or unknowingly. Reports identified him as PG-804-R and later as T-2 and T-14 to disguise his identity, according to declassified FBI reports. He was described in documents as "one of the most active gambling figures who is a close friend of Samuel Mannarino," according to a 1966 report. Bureau censors did a poor job shielding Mannarino's identity, using his name openly in some reports.

Mannarino told an FBI agent during one of their meetings that he introduced to many of the old mafiosi leaders known as "Moustache Petes" because of the handlebar moustaches they wore as he began his climb through the ranks of the Mafia until he became a "made" member in the 1940s. He bragged about knowing Vito Genovese of New York and Sam Giancana of Chicago. He decried the abilities of younger members of the mob because he considered them stupid and unreliable. He said there was "very little proper training for young guys nowadays and there ain't the same kind of discipline there used to be 30 years ago."

He provided details about rivalries between members within the Mannarino organization. He told the agents that he hated Sonny Ciancutti, who worked for his brother Kelly. "I wouldn't be seen walking across the street with that punk." He said if Ciancutti had come up for membership in the Mafia in the 1960s, he never would have been inducted. "He would have been made a member of the cemetery 30 years ago," he told the FBI in a 1966 interview.

Sam Mannarino killed his first person by accident when he struck and killed a pedestrian on a Pittsburgh street in 1927; it was ruled an accident by the coroner. His name resurfaced in the city's underworld in a gangland killing in the New Kensington area in 1934 after Patsy Arabia, a local gambler and bootlegger, went to meet with Sam, Joey Rosa and Willie and Albert Sams despite his wife pleading with him not to leave home because she suspected he was going to be killed.

Anna Arabia knew her husband was a marked man. "I told him…not to go when he put a gun in his pocket. I said, 'Patsy, if you go out there with these men tonight, you're going for a ride.' I know none of them had any use for Patsy because he knew too much about what they've been doing," reported the *Pittsburgh Press* in 1934.

Allegheny County detectives suspected Sam Mannarino was one of the killers because "Sam Mannarino was one of the men with Rosa," according to the *Pittsburgh Post*. Mannarino was not charged in Arabia's murder, but Rosa and Sams were arrested and acquitted after a trial. Sam Mannarino enticed Arabia to a meeting with a job offer at a gambling club if he would work for him. After his murder, Anna Arabia said two men came to her home, pulled out a machine gun and warned her she would be killed if she testified. She testified anyway.

Workers on a construction project in 1947 unearthed the skeletal remains believed to be of a former boxer from Ohio buried in New Kensington that authorities suspected was the victim of a gangland killing a decade earlier. Because the body was found in New Kensington, Sam Mannarino became a suspect. Jimmy Muche was a former pug who worked as a dealer at the notorious mob-run Jungle Inn gambling casino near Youngstown, Ohio. He fought as a welterweight from 1921 until 1930 and won five of his first six bouts, ending his career with nineteen wins, eighteen losses and three draws.

After quitting boxing, he worked as a bodyguard for a Cleveland racketeer and then as a dealer at the Jungle Inn. He was last seen alive on April 23, 1937. Muche reportedly was caught with his hand in the till and was sentenced to death. Police suspected that Muche was killed in Ohio and driven to Pennsylvania, where his body was dumped in New Kensington and covered with lime to speed decomposition. His identity was never confirmed, although there were a few scraps of fabric, eyeglasses and a belt buckle with the letter *M*. No one ever was arrested for Muche's killing, according to an FBI office memo in 1964.

Two mobsters from Cleveland showed up at the home of his wife, Dorothy, and promised "no harm would come to him. My husband is not a hunted criminal and has no reason to leave town for a few days," she said, according to the book *Welcome to the Jungle Inn: The Story of the Mafia's Infamous Gambling Den.*

He told the agents that "when he was much younger, he had participated in several 'hits' and in fact, 'I used to enjoy it,'" according to an interview conducted with Mannarino by Agents Forsyth and William B. Anderson Jr. on April 14, 1964.

The FBI was very interested in the health of the brothers. They learned from Sam's personal physician that he was suffering from colon cancer and was addicted to cocaine. Kelly was described in bureau reports as a "glutton" because of his eating habits. On March 23, 1970, the five-foot, four-inch Mannarino cooked two pigs for friends and the next day suffered a heart attack. When he was discharged from the hospital, he was ordered by his physician to lose weight, a feat that was difficult for a man who had a fondness for chocolate-covered turtles, a candy made with pecans, nuts, chocolate and caramel.

He loved the candy so much that he took over a candy store from the owner who was deep in debt from gambling. Even though the short, stocky, bad-tempered mobster was fifty pounds overweight, he couldn't resist the candy. When he was out of town, he had the candy shipped to him wherever he was staying. Catoris Candies became his base of operations after assuming control of the company from Louis Catoris, who remained with the company to make the candy.

Kelly Mannarino solidified his position in the Mafia by marrying Jean Amato, the daughter of Frank Amato Sr. Jean Amato was another Mafia wife who "had no choice" in her selection of a mate because the union was arranged by her father. Matrimony didn't stop Mannarino from trysts with girlfriends at motels and fathering a child with a secretary in one of his businesses, according to bureau reports. The FBI noted in a 1951 report that Kelly Mannarino had poor taste when it came to women, writing that "he has been observed on numerous occasions in [the] company of girls who would generally be considered homely and unkempt."

Kelly was arrested in 1943 for carrying a concealed weapon by a constable who happened to be one of his friends. The FBI speculated the arrest was a ruse to escape military service because Mannarino and the arresting constable were seen chatting amiably after a judge dropped the charge. The arrest came a week after he was classified 1-A and ordered to report for a physical. Mannarino didn't have to worry about going to war. A military doctor found him to be obese, and an army psychiatrist diagnosed him as having a "constitutional psychopathic inferior personality" and rejected him for military service. The current term for the malady is antisocial personality disorder and is marked by a "lifelong pattern of law-breaking, manipulation, and callous disregard toward others," according to the *Journal of the American Medical Association*.

The Mannarino brothers built a gambling empire that encompassed Westmoreland County, northern Allegheny County and Armstrong County. They also had gambling interests in Cuba, northern West Virginia and eastern Ohio as well as an interest in the Stardust Casino in Las Vegas, according to the *New Kensington Daily Dispatch*. The Stardust was run by their friend Milton Jaffe, who had owned a share of the Pittsburgh Steelers before moving to Nevada.

The brothers were always looking for new ways to make money, as evidenced by their attempt to muscle their way into the Los Angeles rackets before the police forced them to leave the city. Eastern mobsters began arriving in Los Angeles in the late 1940s and began demanding 25 percent of the revenue from nightclubs and restaurants for protection. Captain Lynn White, head of the Los Angeles Police Department's intelligence unit, described the brothers as "pretty tough customers" in a memo to the FBI in 1947.

The FBI and Beverly Hill Police initially suspected that the brothers were behind the unsolved murder of California mobster Bugsy Siegel, who was killed in Beverly Hills on June 27, 1947. Siegel developed the Flamingo Hotel on the Las Vegas Strip but ran afoul of his fellow gangsters because of overspending on construction and rumors that he was skimming money from his mob partners. Siegel was shot in the head as he was meeting with Allen Smiley, who was a friend of Mannarino associate Abe Zeid, who was questioned in the killing.

Jo Jo Mannarino visited Siegel earlier in Las Vegas, seeking a piece of the Flamingo on behalf of his brothers, but Seigel refused to cut them in on a share of the profits. Sam Mannarino also met with Siegel and was rebuffed. Siegel was killed a short time later, but there was no evidence linking the Mannarinos to the murder.

On paper, the brothers appeared to be upstanding citizens. They were members of the Catholic Church and the Holy Name Society. They ran legitimate businesses, helped the needy and were members of the Moose and Elks. Sam served for a time on the board of directors of Citizens General Hospital in New Kensington.

Sam Mannarino spent a considerable amount of time in church, but not for spiritual reasons. He vanished in 1958 as U.S. marshals searched for him so they could serve him with a subpoena to appear before a federal grand jury. Mannarino was holed up on the third floor of the rectory at Mount Saint Peter's Catholic Church, hidden by his close friend and pastor, Monsignor Nichola Fusco, who looked at Sam and Kelly Mannarino as "his boys," according to a report by Special Agent Thomas Forsyth III in 1958.

Although the Mannarinos were members of the parish, the bureau was skeptical that they were practicing Catholics. "[Kelly] Mannarino can hardly be classified as a devout member of the Roman Catholic faith" despite his claims to be "a regular practitioner of that faith," Forsyth added. Kelly Mannarino picked up the tab for Fusco's trips to Rome and when Pope John XXIII was installed, Mannarino paid for Fusco's first-class travel to Rome. Some of Fusco's parishioners objected to his close relationship with the brothers, but Fusco ignored their entreaties, according to a 1959 FBI report.

The relationship between the Mafia and Catholic Church dates back centuries. The church has accommodated mafiosi by allowing them lavish funerals despite their crimes and reputations. In 1993, Pope John Paul II denounced the Mafia, and Pope Francis threatened to excommunicate all Mafia members in 2014.

Fusco baptized mobsters, married them and presided over their funerals in the ornate church that was built with the help of the family of Pittsburgh millionaire Richard Beatty Mellon. R.B., as he was known, died in 1933; his wife, Jennie, died five years later. Their heirs decided to raze the mansion but allowed Fusco to remove parts of the sixty-five-room brownstone to build a new Mount St. Peter's Church in New Kensington.

"Michelangelo had the marble quarries of Italy to build the Sistine Chapel, we had the Mellon mansion to build Mount St. Peter's," said Fusco, according to a history Fusco authored on the history of the parish. Fusco removed thirty tons of steel and sixty-five oak doors from the mansion and had them transported to New Kensington, where the mansion's marble from India and China became altars. Alabaster chandeliers and gold sanctuary lamps lit the interior of St. Peter's.

An FBI agent reported the brothers also curried favor with residents. "Most of the legitimate citizens of the community have received gifts or favors from the Mannarinos or their henchmen and…the Mannarinos move socially across the lines which in most communities would separate them from the legitimate type people," wrote Special Agent Clive G. Matthews in 1963.

"Many legitimate businessmen, who are otherwise active in civic affairs and charitable works, hesitate to cooperate with federal agencies because they are afraid of the Mannarino gang and feel it is so deeply entrenched in the community to dislodge," Matthews added. "New Kensington was perfectly happy with the Mannarinos in charge," added Paul Hess, who said while the mob ruled, crime was not a problem because the brothers would not allow crime to keep gamblers away from the casinos.

Agents approached officials of a drug manufacturing company located across the street from the Mannarino-owned Nu Ken Iron and Steel Company for permission to use a second-floor room to take surveillance photos of the brothers. A company officer refused and was so frightened by the request that his hands shook as he tried to light a cigarette. He later informed the Mannarinos of the bureau's request.

An Alcoa executive who lived across the street from Sam Mannarino agreed to allow agents to use his home to set up a surveillance post on the second floor to photograph Mannarino entering and leaving his house, but the effort proved fruitless. Every time he left his house, he pulled his hat down over his forehead, wore dark glasses and covered his face with a handkerchief as if he knew he was being watched.

"The situation is an excellent example of the obstacles that must be overcome in connection with any violations within the Bureau's jurisdiction in New Kensington which is dominated by the Mannarino gang," complained FBI special agent Richard Gordon Douce in a 1959 report.

New Kensington and other local police departments paid little attention to gambling, especially in New Kensington, because the Mannarinos controlled the mayor, city council and police department. Police officers were barred from conducting raids or making arrests. New Kensington police chiefs claimed they never received any complaints about gambling, even when a city policeman in uniform and two off-duty Pittsburgh police officers were swept up in a raid by the IRS at a notorious gambling haunt, according to the *Pittsburgh Post-Gazette*.

When city police or Westmoreland County detectives staged raids, they were just for show. Then district attorney Richard McCormick, who later became a judge, was in a tough reelection campaign in 1961 and raided a Mannarino casino after the IRS had conducted an earlier raid. The FBI reported the raid was staged because Sonny Ciancutti was ordered to be present at the gambling joint so he could be arrested and the resulting publicity make McCormick look good with voters, according to the *New Kensington Daily Dispatch*.

The Mannarinos ruled their gambling enterprises with an iron hand. Fail to pay your gambling debts and you could expect a beating. Two men were savagely beaten for falling behind in their payments. One man suffered a fractured skull, broken cheekbone and black eyes. Neither man pressed charges, according to the *Daily Dispatch*. The FBI learned from an informant that other deadbeats were taken to an undisclosed location known as "the farm" where they were interrogated by Kelly Mannarino and Sonny Ciancutti. Failure to come up with the money resulted in a beating.

Anybody wanting to hold cards or craps games had to have permission from the brothers and pay them a percentage of the take in order to operate. Jimmy Burgart had been running a lucrative horse room and numbers racket for three decades when the Mannarinos decided in 1960 that Burgart should refer future business to them. Burgart was grossing an estimated $100,000 a year and would lose his commission on bets if he began banking with the Mannarinos. When Burgart refused to cooperate, the word was put out on the street by Mannarino associates that Burgart was unable to cover his wins and saw his business cut in half. Burgart later became an FBI informant, according to bureau reports.

The Mannarinos were able to protect their gambling interests by controlling law enforcement. Pennsylvania State Police commanders who were overly aggressive in staging raids were transferred to posts a distance from their homes. Captain James Maroney told the FBI in 1958 that when he sought a transfer to be commander of the state police barracks in Greensburg, he first had to promise Pennsylvania state senator John Dent, who depended on the Mannarinos for political and financial support, that he would do nothing to disrupt the "Mannarinos gambling interests in New Kensington without first clearing a raid first with the District Attorney for Westmoreland County." Maroney got his transfer.

4
GANGSTERS

The Mannarino organization was made up of men the brothers grew up with and trusted. Willie Sams, according to the FBI, was known as a top handicapper and the "brains" behind their gambling enterprises. Tom Tannas was the city clerk of the neighboring city of Arnold and manager of boxer Ezzard Charles, the two-time heavyweight champ. The FBI labeled Tannas as the bagman for payoffs to politicians.

Sam Mannarino's son-in-law, Victor Carlucci, was a musician, bandleader, beer distributor and wannabe mobster who died of a heart attack in his forties. Abe Zeid, who went by the alias Al Ross, was a reputed killer for the Mannarinos, although his reputation as a mob triggerman may have been exaggerated. Mike Giorano used the alias Nick Jerome. Norman Rothman was a gambler who fronted the brothers at a gambling casino in Havana. Joe Merola was a former used car salesman from Pittsburgh turned jewel thief based in Miami who grew close to the Mannarinos until they discovered he was a government informant.

Daniel "Speedo" Hanna was a dealer and bouncer at Mannarino-run gambling haunts. He served in the U.S. Marines and was wounded during the Battle of Okinawa in World War II. Hanna considered becoming an FBI informant while serving a five-year federal prison term for gunrunning after Sam Mannarino assured him he would never be convicted because the "fix" was in. If he, by chance, was convicted, his family would be taken care of financially, but Mannarino never kept his promise. While Hanna was languishing at the Allenwood honor farm near Lewisburg, Pennsylvania, the FBI interviewed him but were unable to convince him to become an informant despite his unhappiness over Mannarino's failure to keep his promise.

Thomas "Sonny" Ciancutti was a former high school football star who ranked 165 out of a class of 387. His mother, Eleanor Ciancutti, worked as a dealer for the Mannarinos in one of their gambling clubs, and she rued the day they recruited her son because she wanted Sonny to become a lawyer instead of a racketeer.

Ciancutti played football for three years at New Kensington High School. The Ken Hi Red Raiders had a tradition steeped in football and won regional titles in 1946 and 1947, winning twenty-four straight games. The school produced Willie Thrower, the first African American to play quarterback in the NFL, when he was with the Chicago Bears.

The University of Pittsburgh, Rutgers, Duquesne University, North Carolina, Michigan State and Washington and Lee University expressed interest in Ciancutti's football talent, but he enrolled at Washington and Lee; however, he dropped out of school after breaking his ankle in an auto accident. He later attended the University of Pittsburgh

Abe Zeid, who was also known as Al Ross, was the reputed executioner for the Mannarino organization. He was tortured and murdered on the orders of Kelly Mannarino because he was talking with the FBI. *Wikipedia.*

and Duquesne University but dropped out from both schools. He spent less than a year in the U.S. Army and received a medical discharge because of a nervous tic. He held a series of low-level jobs, working at a bowling alley, as a bartender and at a poolroom, according to a 1964 FBI background report.

Ciancutti began working for Kelly Mannarino as an errand boy and then as muscle for Mannarino's loan sharking operations. Ciancutti was a rough customer. He once beat a man senseless in 1961 over a debt as a New Kensington police officer stood nearby and was afraid to intervene and stop the beating. Another gambler was in debt to the Mannarino mob for $18,000, so Sonny confiscated the man's Cadillac. The owner had an extra set of keys and retrieved his car only to have Sonny track him down, beat him and recover the vehicle.

Ciancutti was being groomed to be Mannarino's right-hand man, but he fell in and out of favor, according to the FBI. He liked to drink, gamble, carouse and golf and was a poor manager of one of the mob's gambling enterprises, earning him a brief banishment to Las Vegas.

The brothers bought a scrapyard in 1940 and hired their cronies so they could escape the draft during World War II by claiming they worked in an industry essential to the war effort. Industries used recycled scrap metals to build ships, tanks and airplanes.

The Mannarinos seemed bulletproof. Nothing stuck to the brothers—local and state law enforcement authorities made little progress curbing their criminal enterprises, and they enjoyed the protection of law enforcement from the cop on the beat to judges and Pennsylvania governors. Bookies and gamblers were treated leniently by the courts after they were arrested and punished with small fines. When state troopers raided a gambling casino in Westmoreland County, a judge accused the troopers of acting like the Gestapo in Nazi Germany. *Collier's* magazine published a classic article, "Something's Rotten in the State of Pennsylvania," documenting the unholy alliance between the Mafia and the justice system.

Daniel "Speedo" Hanna was an associate of Sam Mannarino who delivered the shipment of stolen weapons to a rural airstrip. Hanna was a former Marine who was wounded during the Battle of Okinawa in World War II. *Wikipedia.*

Newspapers were incensed by the lenient treatment racketeers received from judges. The *Daily Dispatch* in New Kensington charged that the mayor, police chief and most of the city council were in the pockets of the Mannarinos. Publisher Gene Simon pursued the mob relentlessly. Simon worked as a reporter in the late 1940s for the *Harrisburg Patriot and Evening News*. He married the daughter of Charles Howe, the founder of the *Valley Daily News*, and was president from 1949 until 1976, when Simon sold the company to Gannett.

Reporter Paul Hess's immediate boss was Frank Anderson, a veteran newsman who was born and raised in New Kensington and once worked as a doorman at one of Kelly Mannarino's clubs. Anderson and Mannarino met after World War II, and Anderson developed a cordial relationship with Mannarino, who called Anderson one day to talk about news coverage of New Kensington. "You don't have to worry about any of your reporters being hurt by us," Mannarino told Anderson. Hess said Anderson told him about the conversation, but the newspaper never pulled its punches in coverage of organized crime.

The *Monessen Daily Independent*, another Westmoreland County–based newspaper, wrote that "a cooperative association [existed] between politicians and the underworld for mutual prosperity." The *Uniontown Morning Herald* in neighboring Fayette County editorialized, "It is beyond our conception to understand why the good people of Westmoreland County do not rise up in the name of good government and demand one of two things—law enforcement or impeachment of any and all corrupt county officials."

The brothers' influence extended deeply into the daily fabric of New Kensington's political and social world. They installed their vending and slot machines in bars, restaurants and stores throughout the region; employed an army of bookies; operated gambling dens; and served as a third political party alongside Democrats and Republicans. Kelly Mannarino was overheard joking that if there were two horses in a race, one a Democrat and the other a Republican, it wouldn't matter which horse won because he "owned" them both, wrote Special Agent Richard Gordon Douce, on April 14, 1958.

"It was difficult to gather information against the Mannarinos in those days because people who knew things were afraid to talk," said Forsyth, according to a 1996 interview with the *Greensburg Tribune-Review*.

J. Edgar Hoover ordered his agents in Pittsburgh to install listening devices in the home of Kelly Mannarino or in the office the brothers used at Ken Iron and Steel Company. Hoover routinely ordered the installation of wiretaps without seeking a court order in what was known as "black bag" operations during investigations of the Mafia and Communist Party. Agents used the information gathered from the listening devices and attributed the intel to informants to disguise the fact that the bureau broke the law.

The entry and installation were planned by Special Agent Thomas Forsyth III. After figuring out the best way to get into the office at the scrapyard, teams of agents kept the building under surveillance while other agents tailed Mannarino associates and patrolling New Kensington Police officers to make sure their fellow agents were not caught breaking into the building. The bug was activated on March 6, 1964, and continued until July 22, when the operation was discontinued because it produced nothing incriminating.

"Sam is now spending the greater part of each day at his office.…Samuel Mannerino receives visits in this office on almost a daily basis, some of whom are known to Mannarino or on the fringe of racketeering activities," read a 1964 report from the special agent in charge of the Pittsburgh office to Hoover seeking wiretap authorization.

When the microphone failed to elicit any incriminating information against the Mannarinos, it was decided to send two agents to "prime the pump" by interviewing Sam Mannarino in his office in the hope he would be overheard heard discussing the visit after the agents left. "It is believed Mannarino will almost have to make comments of interest after the departure of the Special Agents," read the report. The visit produced nothing of value. Even though the surreptitious entry was illegal, Forsyth's boss recommended Forsyth receive a letter of commendation for his "diligent and ingenuous work."

The bureau also wanted to install a wiretap in Kelly Mannarino's rural hideaway that he was building outside of New Kensington. Agents obtained the building's floor plans and were going to disguise themselves as workmen and install microphones inside the walls of the unfinished home. But Mannarino outfoxed them. He didn't have any telephones in his retreat and warned associates to never discuss business over the telephone. Instead, Mannarino walked a half mile down the road to use a payphone whenever he needed to call someone.

No place, not even New Kensington, was safe from the mob. In 1979, two men stole a Purolator armored truck in the city netting $660,000 in cash. The vehicle was stolen in front of a bank; the thieves used a key to open the door and simply drove away. They left another $200,000 behind when they abandoned the vehicle a half mile away. One suspect was arrested and sentenced to a decade in prison. A second suspect was never found, and the FBI suspected he may have been the victim of a Mafia hit. The FBI speculated that Kelly Mannarino would never have allowed such a high-profile crime to be committed on his home turf without his approval.

By the late 1960s, agents saw less and less of Kelly Mannarino in New Kensington because he was spending more time at his winter home in the beachfront community of Surfside, Florida, where he frequented the Gold

Coast Restaurant and Lounge owned by his friend Joe Sonken, a former Chicago saloon keeper and bootlegger who moved to Florida, where he operated Mother Kelly's. The FBI suspected Kelly Mannarino was the real owner or a silent partner in the nightclub, which closed in 1948. Sonken then opened the Gold Coast Lounge, which the bureau suspected was financed by Mannarino.

The Gold Coast attracted mobsters like Meyer Lansky, Angelo Bruno of Philadelphia and other top mafiosi from New York City. The Pennsylvania Crime Commission reported Mannarino was seen meeting at the Gold Coast with Buffalo mobster Russell Bufalino, LaRocca and a member of the Genovese crime family from New York. An unlisted telephone behind the bar served as a national message center where Mafia bosses could leave messages.

Mannarino dined on the homemade ravioli and chicken Vesuvio, potatoes and peas roasted in white wine that Sonken was famous for serving, according to 2018 profile in the *Miami New Times*. Sonken and Mannarino were such close friends that when Mannarino died in 1980, Sonken almost "fell apart." The FBI suspected that cookware manufactured by Alcoa that disappeared from the company's New Kensington warehouse ended up in the kitchen at the Gold Coast.

5
"LAS VEGAS OF THE EAST"

It was a busy Saturday night on April 23, 1961, when Dante Bonomi and three other men entered the plush casino hidden in the basement of the Garibaldi Club in New Kensington. The entrance to the Garibaldi was tucked away in an alley and guarded by steel doors. There were no street numbers on the building to mark the address. To gain admittance, a visitor walked down an alley between a furniture store and a grocery before entering the building through a door at street level and then walking down a flight of six steps that ended at a green steel door where a doorman decided whether or not to let you in.

Bonomi started visiting the casino three times a week over several months, placing forty bets on the numbers, the ponies and shooting craps. Bonomi seemed out of place among the other gamblers, and the dealers sensed he was not who he claimed to be, a blue-collar worker who liked to gamble. He asked the names of employees and seemed to be fixated on memorizing the layout of the casino's interior. "I was surprised when I saw the size of the place," he reported, according to the *Pittsburgh Post-Gazette*.

The dealers were right. Bonomi was not a gambler. He was a U.S. Treasury agent working undercover who was brought in by the IRS from New Jersey to infiltrate the casino's operations in preparation for a raid as part of U.S. Attorney General Robert F. Kennedy's war on organized crime. Bonomi later testified at the trial of Willie Sams, Sonny Ciancutti, Frank "Frinkie" Phillips and Mike Giorano, who were convicted and fined a total of $110,000 but avoided going to prison.

New Kensington became a target of FBI and IRS investigations after Kennedy became the nation's top law enforcement officer. IRS agents scoured the city, talking to informants and business owners to learn how the brothers and associates spent their money, and subpoenaed their bank records. They tracked gambling joints and calculated the amount of money gambling generated.

The casino was a cash cow for the Mannarinos generating $2 million a year, according to the IRS. Over $100,000 in wagers exchanged hands every night. Numbers and sports bets brought in $10,000 a day each while craps games generated as much as $75,000 a night. Barbut bets totaled $1,500 an hour. The casino also served as a numbers bank, where the daily gross from bettors was stored with amounts ranging from $10,000 to $12,000. The casino even had its own transportation system known as "luggers," who drove gamblers from Pittsburgh to New Kensington.

Two other undercover IRS agents had infiltrated the gambling operation along with Bonomi. One evening things got dicey as dealers grew suspicious of Bonomi. Agent Edward Cassidy sensed trouble and wiped his forehead with a handkerchief—a prearranged warning signal—for Bonomi to get out immediately. A third undercover agent, Charles Daverio, saw the signal and headed for the door. Suspicious casino employees followed the trio outside as they walked to a car and left New Kensington.

When Bonomi showed up the next day, August 24, 1961, at 5:00 p.m., a doorman refused to let him enter. "You're not getting in anymore," according to an account in the *Pittsburgh Post-Gazette*. Just then, two flatbed trucks arrived with dozens of IRS agents and deputy U.S. marshals hiding behind canvas tarps. The raiding party came storming into the Garibaldi, pushing past the doorman, smashing through two doors and bursting into the casino. Among the gamblers were a uniformed New Kensington patrolman and two Pittsburgh police officers.

When agents began escorting the suspects outside, a crowd of five hundred surrounded them and began heckling and jostling the federal agents. The New Kensington police were called to help, but a dispatcher said there were no officers available, so state police came to the rescue. The incident triggered an editorial rebuke from the *New Kensington Daily Dispatch* berating Police Chief John Bordonaro and Mayor Raymond Gardlock:

> *To offer the excuse as city hall has done that the police department did not know what was happening is ridiculous and no one in his right mind will believe it. You can be sure that police officials knew all along*

what was happening and that the failure to send officers to the scene was deliberate. And they also knew all along of the existence of the casino and yet never raised a finger against it. To ask why they failed to act is senseless—everyone knows. This glaring failure could well have had tragic consequences. Some of the crowd sided with the gamblers who had been arrested and became unruly. The federal agents did their best to preserve order when it seemed they might have to draw their guns to protect themselves. Had they been forced to do this there is no telling what might have happened and no one would have been to blame for the possible bloody consequences but Chief [John] Bordonaro. The only logical explanation for the failure of proper police officials to send men to the scene is the close ties that exist between certain police officials and the mob. These officials did not intend to make anything that even looked like a hostile move against their law-breaking pals.

Bonomi, who served as a paratrooper with the Eleventh Airborne in the South Pacific during World War II, was a key witness in a federal trial against four Mannarino underlings who were convicted of gambling. The FBI later learned that a contract had been put out on Bonomi's life. "Bonomi is a dead man. A contract has been issued on Bonomi's life. He is an Italian and therefore he is a traitor," wrote the special agent in charge of the Pittsburgh field office to J. Edgar Hoover on March 1, 1963.

FBI special agent Thomas Forsyth III, who spent years investigating the Mannarinos, said the IRS raid was ill-advised and poorly planned because it prevented the bureau from gathering further intelligence. The FBI said it had a highly placed informant within the Mannarino organization, and the raid made it difficult for the informant to gather more information on the brothers, who now were on their guard.

"When the raid occurred, the result was that the Mannarinos ordered a moratorium on all alleged illegal activities," Forsyth wrote in a memo. "There is so little happening in the New Kensington area that there is very little information that can be obtained and furnished to Pittsburgh office."

U.S. Attorney General Nicholas Katzenbach singled out the New Kensington Police Department for failing to move against the casino despite their knowledge that the Mafia was operating a casino in the club. "We know this was done with the acquiescence of city officials. Why did they not take action?" reported the *Pittsburgh Post-Gazette*.

The Garibaldi raid made the brothers paranoid. Kelly Mannarino moved the operation to another location and increased security. Lookouts armed with two-way radios stood on the roofs of buildings near their gambling haunts ready to relay a warning of an impending raid to another watchdog who sat in a car outside the building with a radio ready to alert the doorman.

Kelly Mannarino ordered New Kensington police officers to tail FBI agents whenever they were in the city to see where they went and to whom they talked. Listening devices were installed in the rooms of the Kenmar Hotel where agents sometimes stayed, according to an FBI report. An informant told the FBI that the Mannarinos had a Bell Telephone operator reporting to them about any calls made by residents to the FBI or IRS in Pittsburgh. The FBI learned in 1957 that Sam Mannarino was searching for an individual who had called the FBI to provide information on Sam and Kelly. He wanted to find the caller to "split his head open," according to the report.

The faces of the brothers were unfamiliar to the FBI in the early days of their investigations, so agents scoured newspaper morgues and commercial photography studios looking for pictures. Commercial photographers were reluctant to help, claiming they did not keep the negatives from weddings, baptisms and family gatherings. Agents selected a building across the street from Mannarino's office in the Ken Iron and Steel Company as a hiding spot to surreptitiously photograph the brothers' comings and goings. Agents approached the head of the company and asked permission to establish a surveillance post. At first, the official was eager to cooperate with the FBI but had second thoughts out of fear of reprisals and warned the Mannarinos about the bureau's request.

"This situation is an excellent example of the obstacles that must be overcome in connection with any violation within in the Bureau's jurisdiction in New Kensington which is dominated completely by the Mannarino gang," lamented Special Agent Richard Gordon Douce.

Nothing, not even death, was allowed to interfere with gambling. On the night of December 3, 1959, Tom Gallian was on a hot streak while playing a game of skin, a card game where players bet on each card. The betting starts out small but quickly climbs to larger amounts. That night, bets started at $10 a card, but the pot grew larger and larger until it reached $5,000. Gallian wanted to keep playing, but he needed $1,700 to remain in the game, so he borrowed the money from his cousin Sonny Ciancutti, a Mannarino shylock, whose mother, Eleanor, was the dealer and Gallian's aunt.

Gallian was a card away from winning or losing a small fortune. He lost and fell face down on the table, dead of a heart attack at forty-three. "The other players merely lifted his head, observed that he appeared to be dead and proceeded to finish the hand they were playing," read a 1959 FBI report. Gallian's body was carried out of the club and dumped several blocks away so his death would not be tied to the club. His death certificate indicated he died of a heart attack while walking on the street.

Some gamblers got into such deep debt at the Garibaldi that they stole money from their employers to cover their losses. John Konowal Jr. was the treasurer of the credit union at Jones and Laughlin Steel Corp. in Aliquippa, north of Pittsburgh. He stole $75,000 to cover the $42,000 in gambling losses he incurred at the casino and wrote personal checks to cover his debts and then transferred money from the credit union to his bank account, according to a statement he gave to Special Agents Thomas Forsyth III and J. Edward Madvay.

"I started out small and expected to replace the money," he told the agents. Konowal later was indicted by a federal grand jury, convicted and sentenced to forty months in prison. The money he stole ended up in the pockets of Kelly Mannarino. "It is my belief, based on casual conversations with other gambling patrons in New Kensington…that the gambling joints in the Garibaldi Building…were controlled by Kelly Mannarino of New Kensington," read Konowal's statement.

Five New Kensington bank employees were charged with embezzling money from banks in 1951 to pay gambling debts. One employee stole $650,000, claiming he was going to use the money to buy the bank where he worked even though the institution wasn't for sale. Another teller confessed to the FBI that he spent $300,000 to pay off gambling debts, but when the mob learned he was stealing from his employer, they forced him to continue stealing or they would expose him. The teller was sentenced to a decade in prison and told the FBI he kept taking money because he "lived in mortal fear" of the Mafia.

Residents began joking about the thefts: "'I got the old lady a cleaning job down at the bank,' said one man to another. 'But that doesn't pay much,' the second man replied. 'Oh, she's a teller. Cleans up a little every day,'" reported the *Pittsburgh Post-Gazette*.

Even the police weren't immune from the greedy mobsters. When the Fraternal Order of Police in the neighboring city of Lower Burrell held a picnic, the police chief recruited dealers working for Kelly Mannarino to run gambling at the event. Using marked cards and loaded dice, the FBI said the card sharks took the cops for $1,500. By the time the police realized they had been cheated, the gamblers had fled.

Liberty Theater in downtown New Kensington was one of five theaters in the once bustling downtown. *Library of Congress.*

Gambling helped make New Kensington prosper. The downtown was a busy commercial district in the 1950s. The streets were filled with shoppers making purchases at the several department stores, watching films at the five movie theaters or eating at restaurants or hotels that occupied several blocks. "You couldn't walk along the sidewalk on a Saturday night....It was really a chore...because you couldn't get anywhere. You were just in crowd all the time," said Gino Marotto in an interview with *Pennsylvania Folklife* magazine.

Journalist Paul Hess said downtown New Kensington was "busy, busy, busy" when the Mafia ran the city. "There were a number of large department stores, hardware stores, jewelry stores, children's and baby clothes shops. The streets were packed," he told the author.

If you committed a crime downtown, having the police arrest you was the least of your worries. A teenage purse snatcher committed a series of thefts and wouldn't stop until a message was sent via an intermediary from "the boys" to stop or else, recalled Hess. The thefts stopped. "The mob wouldn't tolerate crime downtown," he added.

The Mannarinos owned New Kensington. They controlled the mayor's office, the police department and city council. Sam Mannarino once boasted to an FBI agent that the brothers wielded such absolute power over municipal government that "no one in this city gets any appointment to local police or Liquor Board or anything else unless we clear them."

Hess said reporting on New Kensington was difficult but exciting. He rubbed shoulders with racketeers and had a cordial relationship with some of them. Others he steered clear off because of their violent nature. Few individuals dared challenge the brothers' control. One who did was Jim Kelly, whose real name was Dmitrius Petros Califerous. He was a bookie who ran a shoeshine parlor in New Kensington. In 1956, he backed a challenger of incumbent Mayor Raymond Gardlock and was told by Kelly Mannarino he could no longer take bets because he had supported the wrong candidate. Kelly confronted Kelly Mannarino and told him to check with Gardlock.

"I don't call anyone because I'm the mayor of this town and what I say goes," said an angry Mannarino, who glanced at an array of guns hanging on a wall. Jim Kelly also looked threateningly at the guns and said sarcastically,

Postcards of downtown New Kensington in the 1950s during the Mafia's heyday. *Peoples Library.*

"Okay Mr. Mayor. Guns shoot both ways." Kelly Mannarino laughed and called the New Kensington police chief, telling him to "let the crazy Greek alone and that everything had been settled." Jim Kelly related details of the meeting to FBI agent Thomas Forsyth III in 1959.

The brothers had the clout to override decisions by elected leaders. In 1958, the city council considered raising local taxes, which was opposed by the chamber of commerce. A chamber official met with Kelly Mannarino, and the next day Mayor Gardlock announced that the city council was abandoning a tax hike.

When the police department was scouting for a location to open a substation in downtown New Kensington, it rented a building from a company owned by Kelly Mannarino, according to a report by the Pennsylvania Crime Commission. When Westmoreland County district attorney Earl Keim wanted to run for judge, the Mannarinos sent word to Keim that he would remain as district attorney "where he could do the most good for the Mannarino organization," according to a 1958 FBI report.

In addition to choosing candidates for elective office, Sam and Kelly recommend individuals for city, county and state jobs and dictated to tavern owners what brands of beer to buy and who to buy it from. The FBI received an anonymous letter postmarked May 8, 1958, from a tavern owner complaining how Sam Mannarino forced tavern owners to buy a certain brand of beer from City Beverage, which was owned by his son-in-law Victor Carlucci.

"I and other tavern owners are being forced to buy our beer from City Beverage or face the loss of our cigarette, pinball and music machines.… The cheap beer we are forced to buy is causing us to lose trade. We cannot complain to local police of Liquor Board [because] we know that Mannarino controls them. I thought we lived in a free country but New Kensington has its own Khrushchev," read the letter sent to Special Agent Richard Gordon Douce. In 1961, Special Agent Clive Matthews submitted a report to FBI headquarters about the influence the Mannarinos wielded in the region:

> *This was an example of the far-reaching influence of the Mannarino organization in Pennsylvania political circles. In most communities persons commonly regarded as criminals, hoodlums, or racketeers, are looked down upon by the legitimate business people. It is not so, however, with the Mannarino group. There is hardly a person in the New Kensington area who is engaged in legitimate business who cannot recall anywhere from one*

to many [sic] *legitimate dealings had with the Mannarino group to the profit of the legitimate businessmen. Also, most of the legitimate citizens of the community have received gifts or favors from the Mannarinos or their henchmen and that the Mannarinos move socially across lines which in most communities would separate them from the legitimate type people.*

The Mannarinos handpicked New Kensington police chiefs to ensure the protection of their gambling enterprises. Daniel Zeloyle was known as the city's "indestructible cop" for surviving decades in the city's rough-and-tumble world of mob-infested politics, according to the *Pittsburgh Post-Gazette*. He served as police chief three times in his thirty-seven years on the force because he was the favorite of the brothers.

Zeloyle served during the golden age of the rackets in the city from 1928 to 1942, when the Mannarino brothers ascended to power. He survived other changes in administration and remained police chief. Zeloyle oversaw prostitution, which "probably became a municipal operation," and once proclaimed that gambling and prostitution should be legalized as a deterrent to violent crime according to an investigation by the *Pittsburgh Post-Gazette*.

The FBI reported in 1959 that the money Zeloyle received from the Mannarinos enabled him to buy a 157-acre farm in Butler County where he raised chickens and dairy cattle. His legal residence was in Butler County, nearly thirty miles from New Kensington, but he voted in Westmoreland County, where he used the residence of a relative as his legal address.

He sold the eggs his chickens produced in New Kensington for eighty cents a dozen while the market price at the time was forty cents and reduced his transportation costs by using police officers and patrol cars to shuttle the eggs from Butler County to Westmoreland County. When one of his officers wrecked a police car in Butler County, Zeloyle had the wreck towed to New Kensington and reported the accident happened in the city, reported the *Post-Gazette*.

Zeloyle died in 1958 of a heart attack. His wife, Pauline, asked an FBI informant, believed to be Sam Mannarino, how much protection money her husband had received over the years. He told her Zeloyle received $250,000, but his wife had no idea where her husband had stashed the cash. "She was not blind to his corrupt activities and shared the knowledge that he had buried at least one-half million dollars but he would not share the location of his hiding place with her," reported the FBI after Zeloyle's funeral.

Pauline Zeloyle, along with her son, daughter and son-in-law, scoured the farm looking for the money. They believed the late chief buried the money in a milk can somewhere on the property, but they never found the cache. His daughter said before her father died, he was frantic to get out of bed and had to be restrained "because he kept repeating that he had to get up and go out at the farm to do something he considered very important."

More than six hundred mourners turned out for Zeloyle's funeral. Mingling among the grave diggers waiting for the service to end was Sam Mannarino dressed in workman's clothes. Mannarino was being sought at the time by the government to appear before a federal grand jury and suspected FBI agents had staked out the funeral service hoping to serve him with a subpoena. The funeral home allowed two FBI agents to pose as employees, and they joined the funeral procession from the church to the cemetery hoping to spot Mannarino.

Zeloyle was succeeded as chief by John Bordonaro, who "has long been the personal choice of Kelly Mannarino," read an FBI memorandum. Agents placed little trust in sharing or seeking information from him about gambling because Bordonaro "would go to any extreme to avoid any cooperation with FBI and would not hesitate to suppress evidence" of federal laws. He "is completely dominated by the Mannarino organization and Kelly Mannarino in particular."

Bordonaro was ruthless. He was accused of railroading a New Kensington resident for assault after then captain Bordonaro barged into the home of Harry Truitt Jr. and arrested him without a warrant on a misdemeanor. The incident happened during a labor dispute when three pickets got into a scuffle outside a city business. When police arrived, the pickets sought refuge at Truitt's office, where he operated a business making false teeth. Bordonaro burst into the office to arrest the men and got into a scuffle with Truitt over the use of the telephone. Truitt brushed Bordonaro's arm, and the captain claimed Truitt had assaulted him.

Bordonaro arrested Truitt, a critic of the New Kensington mob and city officials. Truitt was convicted and sentenced by Westmoreland County judge John O'Connell to the Allegheny County Workhouse.

The Pennsylvania Supreme Court overturned Truitt's conviction and ordered a new trial citing the introduction of irrelevant testimony and Bordonaro's arrest of Truitt and search of his home without warrants, according to an opinion written by Justice Allen Stearne. Justice Horace Stern concurred, adding that Judge O'Connell allowed the jury to hear "highly inflammable personal attacks" against Truitt that had no relevance to the charges. A new trial was held in a neighboring county. Truitt was convicted again, but this time the judge suspended his sentence.

The Mafia's influence reached the state capital in Harrisburg and the halls of Congress through its ties to Governors James Duff, John Fine, George Leader and David Lawrence and Congressmen John Dent and Gus Kelley, who represented parts of Westmoreland County. FBI files reveal that when Dent was a Pennsylvania state senator, he received political and financial support from the Mannarinos before he was elected to Congress in 1958. Kelley's link to the mob was through an aide, Monessen mayor Hugo Parente, who protected the rackets in the southern portion of Westmoreland County. Kelly Mannarino paid for a party for Governor George Leader in 1958 that was hosted by New Kensington mayor Ray Gardlock. When the Mannarinos' mother died, then-mayor David Lawrence visited the family home to offer his condolences, surprising neighbors, who reported the sighting to the FBI. Political races were financed by bookies who were ordered by the Mannarinos to buy as many as one hundred tickets each to Democratic Party fundraisers during primary and general elections.

William Nowe was a mysterious player in Westmoreland County politics until he was killed in an auto accident in 1957. Nowe was a power in the Westmoreland County Republican Party and was associated with Kelly Mannarino. He also was friends with the county's three judges: Edward Bauer, Richard Laird and John O'Connell.

Nowe maintained box seats at Forbes Field for Pirate baseball games and on opening day each year hosted the judges. After the games, Nowe entertained them and other county politicians at a cocktail party at the swank Schenley Hotel. He was known as "Mr. Republican" in Westmoreland County and was described as a "shadowy and almost legendary figure," by the *Pittsburgh Post-Gazette.*

Nowe was killed on his way to the Westmoreland County Courthouse after

Westmoreland County judge Edward Bauer sentenced racketeers to lenient sentences and once delivered tongue lashing to Pennsylvania State Troopers after they raided a mob-run gambling club. *Pennsylvania House of Representatives.*

his car was sideswiped by an oncoming truck. The FBI learned that after Nowe's body arrived at the funeral home, Kelly Mannarino showed up and demanded the undertaker return $6,000 that Mannarino said Nowe was carrying. The FBI speculated that the money was earmarked as a payoff for the judges. Mannarino knew exactly where Nowe had concealed the money, but the county coroner already had seized the cash. The FBI received a report from an informant that Nowe's death was no accident and that he had been run off the road and into the path of the truck by someone connected to Mannarino.

"No political figure in Westmoreland County has received less publicity than Bill Nowe," read a profile of Nowe in the *Pittsburgh Post-Gazette* in 1952. "Even the men he backs or opposes for office know little about him except that he delivers on election day."

Newspapers were incensed by the judicial treatment of racketeers. The *Daily Dispatch* in New Kensington and its publisher Gene Simon continued to pursue the mob, urged residents to call the FBI and IRS with any information they had on the mob and documented the activities of the Mannarinos, especially after Kelly Mannarino attended the 1957 Mafia summit meeting in New York.

6

BAD BUSINESS

In an old barn on the outskirts of New Kensington, Pennsylvania, far from the prying eyes of the FBI and IRS, hundreds of slot machines sat collecting dust. The idle machines were owned by the Mannarino brothers, who were losing $15,000 a week because they were forced to remove them from bars, restaurants, poolrooms and private clubs throughout the city and adjoining towns lest they be seized by state or federal law enforcement. They had no choice. The federal courts ruled that the slots were illegal because they were gambling devices and could not be transported from state to state. Troopers had seized and destroyed two hundred machines during a 1951 raid, costing the Mannarinos more than $100,000.

The Gambling Devices Act of 1962 made it illegal to manufacture, own or sell slot machines, so the Mannarinos shipped two thousand of their machines to Cuba, where they were placed in the Sans Souci casino outside gambling-crazy Havana to cater to American tourists. Cuban president Fulgencio Batista had come to their rescue by granting the Mannarinos a concession to operate in Cuba. Slot machines, jukeboxes and pinballs proved to be a lucrative revenue source for the Mafia because the odds against winning favored the mob. The machines also had a "reflex unit" installed inside that constantly adjusted the odds of winning to protect the house against major losses, according to a 1964 article in the *Journal of Crime and Criminology*.

The top mafiosi in Pittsburgh all owned vending machine companies as business fronts. The Mannerinos operated S & S Vending along with Nu Ken

Novelty. John LaRocca controlled four firms, the Coin Machine Distributing Company, Rockola Juke Box Company, L & G Amusement Company and Duquesne Vending. Mobster Tony Ripepi ran the Keystone Music Company. Domenick Anzalone, who controlled the rackets in southern Westmoreland County and in neighboring Fayette County, was a partner in the Machine Novelty Company.

LaRocca underboss Mike Genovese appeared before a U.S. Senate Rackets Committee and was accused of using threats and violence to expand his slot machine and pinball racket in the Pittsburgh area. Genovese was a partner in L&G Amusement Company. Even Arthur J. Rooney Sr., the founder of the Pittsburgh Steelers, owned a company, Penn Mint, that distributed slot machines on Pittsburgh's Northside in an arrangement worked out with the Mannarinos. Rooney placed his machines north of the Allegheny River while the Mannarinos controlled the south shore. The vending companies ostensibly provided machines for cigarette and candy sales but were also used to distribute slots, pinball machines and jukeboxes, which were very profitable.

The Pennsylvania Crime Commission reported in 1977 that the state was flooded with gambling devices ranging from slots to punchboards and illegal lottery tickets. The commission discovered more than 6,300 cartons of gambling-related materials were shipped interstate to Pennsylvania—mainly from Chicago—that had a street market value of $53 million.

The cash the machines generated made laundering illegal profits easier because tracing coins was difficult compared to tracking paper currency. Players didn't report taxes on their winnings, and owning a vending company gave racketeers the appearance that they were running a legitimate business and a way to report some of their income to the IRS.

The slots generated money for bribes to pay off police, judges and politicians. When Westmoreland County judges demanded a bigger cut of protection money, the Mannarinos deducted ten dollars from each of the machines they owned to pacify the greedy jurists, according to a May 7, 1958 FBI report. "That way Sam Mannarino and his brother Gabriel have been able to control politicians and operate openly in Westmoreland County without fear or interference by the state and local police," reported FBI agent Thomas Forsyth III.

The first half of the money from the machines was split evenly with the owner of the business where the machines were installed. The second half was listed as the gross for tax purposes. FBI director J. Edgar Hoover, who liked to bet on horses, told a session of the Committee to

Investigate Organized Crime in Interstate Commerce in 1951 that "the local overlord of gambling is an all-powerful figure in his community," according to his testimony.

The revenue was the mob's bread and butter for a time. Gangsters tried to get around the law by claiming the machines were for amusement only, but players could cash in their winnings rather than accumulate free games, which invalidated claims the slots were strictly for entertainment.

Most slot and pinball machines and jukeboxes made in the United States were manufactured in Chicago, according to a U.S. Senate committee—known as the Kefauver Committee after Senator Estes Kefauver—that investigated the shipment of gambling devices across state lines in 1951. One of the largest manufacturing companies was Filben Manufacturing of Chicago, founded by William Filben in the windy city in the 1940s. Filben signed a deal with Rock-Ola Manufacturing Group to produce ten thousand jukeboxes and transferred the rights to the patents to Rock-Ola.

Mannarino also reached a deal with Filben to make jukeboxes in 1947 but never inquired about the patents. Sam arrived in Chicago with two bodyguards toting $300,000 in cash in a brown paper bag for engineering and retooling work, according to FBI accounts. Then he ponied up another $300,000 to make a pilot run of five thousand machines and another $600,000 to begin full production. Before production could start, Rock-Ola sued Filben, claiming it held nontransferable rights to the patents awarded by Filben, which prevented Mannarino from using them. The courts agreed with Rock-Ola, leaving Mannarino literally holding the bag, according to a lawsuit.

Sam Mannarino had no head for business. The Filben debacle was just one of several money-losing schemes he engaged in. He invested in United Dryer Sales and Service, which was going to build automatic hand dryers in restrooms. The firm was founded in 1953 but dissolved three years later. His financial losses forced him to sell real estate that he owned in Las Vegas and Florida on the cheap. He tried to interest investors in a company to manufacture speakers for drive-in movie theaters that also went bust.

In a report by Special Agent Forsyth dated October 26, 1961, Sam was characterized as a "real nut who falls for all sorts of crazy schemes to make money. At times he almost appears senile," and "is always ready to listen to any kind of business deal, and he almost always ends up as the patsy since the deals very rarely are successful and he usually loses his investment."

The Mannarinos' investment in the Sans Souci was short-lived. They claimed they lost money because the Cuban employees they were forced to hire were lazy and stole money from the machines. But the Sans Souci had to compete with larger, more lavish venues controlled by their fellow mobsters, and the truth was the brothers were not smart enough to run a gambling casino said the FBI in its reports.

Norman Rothman was the Mannarinos' man in Havana managing the gaming tables and slot machines until a scandal engulfed the Sans Souci, tarnishing the casino's reputation and keeping gamblers away. Cubileto is a game played

Chart showing the points a gambler could earn by playing razzle-dazzle. Few if any players ever won. *Wikipedia.*

with odds of one in a thousand against winning. Americans referred to the game as "razzle-dazzle," and it fleeced American tourists of thousands of dollars. The game is played with marbles and a wooden tray filled with small holes and marked with numbers. The marbles are rolled from a cup onto the numbers, which are tallied and checked against a chart to see how many points the players earn toward a prize, which is seldom awarded. Razzle-dazzle is a complicated game in which a player is enticed by the operator to double his bets for a better chance at winning.

California attorney Dana C. Smith, a friend and political fundraiser of then U.S. Senator Richard Nixon, lost $4,200 playing the game. Smith wrote a check to cover his losses, and then, angry at being cheated, he canceled payment on the check. Norman Rothman sued Smith in the United States, but other gamblers who wrote checks to cover their gambling losses also stopped payment, leaving Rothman holding $500,000 in debt, according to a 1953 report sent to Hoover from the FBI legal attaché at the American Embassy in Havana.

Sam and Kelly Mannarino, along with John LaRocca, were considered by J. Edgar Hoover to be among the top mafiosi in the United States, even though their names were not as well-known as other major Mafia leaders. LaRocca and Kelly Mannarino were among the attendees flushed by police from the mob summit in Apalachin, New York, in 1957 that put the word *Mafia* in the public lexicon. Hoover ordered agents in Pittsburgh to investigate them. "Investigation should be complete and thorough, and every lead should be promptly run out to its legal conclusions," wrote Hoover to the special agent in charge of the Pittsburgh field office in 1958.

FBI agents dug deep into their lives. They studied the history of the Pittsburgh Mafia and developed informants among bookies, state lawmakers, prostitutes, gamblers, businessmen, bankers, physicians and the clergy. Agents illegally planted listening devices in one of their businesses hoping to develop evidence that would lead to their arrest and prosecution. They delved into their personal lives, their marriages, their sexual peccadillos, surreptitiously photographed them and their associates and studied their financial records looking for ways to nail them for tax evasion.

Special Agents Thomas Forsyth and Richard Gordon Douce, along with IRS agents, spent years in New Kensington trying to penetrate the Mannarino organization. Their names appear on countless reports during their years in the Pittsburgh field office. Before joining the FBI, Forsyth was a bombardier during World War II and worked as an agent in Chicago and San Francisco before being transferred to Pittsburgh, where he was the supervisor of the Organized Crime Unit. He retired from the bureau in 1975 and became a private investigator and later was a special investigator for the U.S. State Department. After Douce retired, he earned a doctorate in psychology and became a forensic psychologist.

Forsyth and Douce were aware of the Mannarinos' violent nature and always noted in their reports a warning about their fascination with guns and violence. Their associates were also violent men. Johnny Fontana was Kelly's trusted lieutenant and bodyguard, who once confronted Douce, warning him to stay out of New Kensington.

"Are you satisfied now—is the FBI satisfied now that the God damn town is closed down?" said Fontana. Douce took the statement as a threat. "I like you, but I can't be a friend of yours; you're on one side. I'm on the other side." Douce ended his October 2, 1958 report with a warning: "Fontana would if circumstances warranted, and if ordered by Gabriel Mannarino, carry out the assination [sic] of any member of law enforcement, including Special Agents of the FBI."

7

PEARL OF THE ANTILLES

In the 1950s, Cuba was a picturesque playground with beautiful weather, pristine golf courses, racetracks, famous bars and restaurants. It was the home of the daiquiri, a rum-based drink named after a mine near Santiago de Cuba. Havana had a four-mile stretch of sun-drenched white sandy beaches known as the Playa del Este, east of the city. Tourists attended cockfights in the afternoon, watched a jai alai match at the Fronton Jai Alai or played the horses at the Oriental Park racetrack. Visitors enjoyed a hedonistic lifestyle, as the city filled with rich Americans who flocked to the mob-run gambling casinos only a ninety-minute flight from Miami.

But the Mannarino brothers weren't attracted to the turquoise-colored water of the Atlantic Ocean, Gulf of Mexico or Caribbean Sea that surrounded the island. They were drawn to the clink of chips sliding across green felt tables, the fan of wads of cash, the sweep of the croupier's rake and the clicking revolutions of a roulette wheel and slots machines in casinos filled with women dressed in elegant gowns and men in white dinner jackets. Cuban dictator Fulgencio Batista welcomed the mob to Cuba, fulfilling a dream of the mob's financial genius, Meyer Lansky, of making Cuba a gambler's paradise unfettered by the law and with the freedom to make millions beyond the prying eyes of the FBI and IRS.

Cuba was referred to as the "Pearl of the Antilles" because of its natural resources of gold, wood and sugar cane. The island shared the title with Haiti. The Antilles comprised the Greater and Lesser Antilles. The Greater Antilles consisted of the Caymans, Cuba, Haiti and the Dominican Republic,

Jamaica and Puerto Rico. The Leeward Islands, the Bahamas and Turks and Caicos comprised the Lesser Antilles.

The center of Havana nightlife was the Tropicana, which opened in 1939 along with the Montmarte and Sans Souci. The floor shows at the Tropicana featuring nearly naked women drew major entertainers, beautiful women and mafiosi. The Tropicana was owned by Martin Fox, but the gambling was under the control of Santo Trafficante Jr. Slot machines—*traganiqueles* in Spanish—were illegal in Cuba, but Batista feigned ignorance of their presence because he received 50 percent of the cash the machines generated and the activities were overseen by his brother-in-law Roberto Fernandez Miranda, who made sure Batista wasn't cheated.

The Sans Souci opened after World War I and was located seven miles outside of Havana. It resembled a Spanish villa with arched openings, a red tile roof and an outdoor stage surrounded by lush gardens. A brochure invited tourists "to stroll in the starlit night through the sweet-scented romantic gardens that surround the San Souci. Dance beneath a Latin moon to the languid music of two top orchestras," according to the 1956 edition of *Cabaret Yearbook*.

Lefty Clark, whose real name was William G. Buschoff, built the Riviera Hotel and Casino in Las Vegas and then later took over management of the Sans Souci after the Mannarinos sold their interest to Trafficante and spent $1 million remodeling the club. Clark had ties to the Mafia in Detroit and to the Purple Gang, a group of Jewish racketeers who were allied with the Mafia.

A night on the town in Havana began with cocktails at the bars along the busy Obispo, a well-traveled Havana venue. A twenty-cent cab ride took you for more drinks at the Floridita Café, where Ernest Hemingway liked to carouse, and then onto La Zaragozana for dinners of prawns, cuttlefish or paella, a mixture of oysters, shrimp, chicken, pork, rice, peas and peppers. Then it was onto a night of gambling in elegant game rooms at the casinos, according to a travel feature in a 1941 edition of the *New York Times*.

While the Mafia saw Havana as a gambler's paradise, Fidel Castro viewed the city as "the brothel of the Western Hemisphere." The nightclubs staged erotic sex shows with beautiful women wearing nothing more than feathers and sequins while simulating sex acts with male partners. There were 270 brothels operating in Havana that employed more than eleven thousand prostitutes catering to horny Americans.

Movie stars, celebrities and politicians were also drawn to Havana's nightlife. Kirk Douglas, Marlon Brando, George Raft, Susan Hayward and Marlene Dietrich were regular visitors. Senators John F. Kennedy and

Richard Nixon came to the island. To lure tourists, the mob hired Frank Sinatra, Tony Martin, Nat King Cole, Denise Darcel, Liberace, Edith Piaf, Sarah Vaughan, Harry Belafonte and Dorothy Dandridge to perform at their nightclubs.

Cuba had long been a haven for racketeers, bootleggers and gamblers since Prohibition because a succession of presidents, government lackeys, the army generals and police officials were corrupt. Smugglers ran rum, sugar and molasses from the island into the United States to supply distillers with the ingredients to furnish bootleg liquor for sale to alcohol-starved Americans. Lucky Luciano and Lansky turned Havana into the "Empress city of organized crime," according to the *Cold War in South Florida*, a study published by the National Parks Service in 2004.

Cuba became a destination for the rich, powerful and corrupt and attracted wealthy Americans and bootleggers during the Great Depression. The Mafia decamped to the island in the 1940s, establishing a foothold with the help of Batista, who was then a sergeant in the Cuban army. Batista was a "mulatto" *macheterosi*, a sugarcane cutter, and received a limited education. He joined the army and worked as a stenographer, rising to the rank of sergeant. He staged a military uprising in 1933 known as the "Revolt of the Sergeants" that brought him to power as the military ruler of Cuba from 1933 until 1944, when he retired and moved to Florida.

Racketeers took advantage of the post–World War II economic boom to build a gambling empire and transformed the island into a "mistress of pleasure, the lush and opulent goddess of delight that existed from 1952 to 1959," wrote *Cabaret Quarterly* magazine in 1956. At a 1946 summit meeting of the top Mafia bosses in Havana called by Lansky and Lucky Luciano, the mobsters decided they needed the authoritarian Batista back in power because of the political instability. He was persuaded to return to Cuba and staged a coup in 1952.

To Castro, the Mafia was just another foreign occupier, a part of a cycle begun when Diego Velazquez de Cuellar settled there in 1511. Cuba had been governed by Spain until the Spanish-American War. The United States ruled Cuba from 1899 until 1902, when Cuba was granted its independence. Congress approved the Platt Amendment granting Cuba a new Cuban constitution but with the caveat that the United States had the right to intervene in the island's internal affairs. Internal bickering among political parties in 1906 saw American troops return, but they were withdrawn three years later. A series of presidents governed from 1909 until 1925, making unsuccessful attempts at social reform.

American companies, among them United Fruit, AT&T and General Motors, dominated the island's businesses and industries. U.S. firms controlled 40 percent of raw sugar production, 50 percent of railroads and 90 percent of telephone and electrical service along with shipping and nickel mining, according to a 1964 study by the Rand Corporation. Cuba ranked fifth in per capita income in the Western Hemisphere and third in life expectancy.

Many Cubans owned automobiles, making the island second in car ownership and first in the ownership of television sets. It had a literacy rate of 76 percent and ranked eleventh in the number of physicians per capita. By the late 1950s, Cuba had become one of the leading economies in Latin America because of its sugar industry, which accounted for four-fifths of its exports, but the Cuban people had no control over their future because the United States controlled the economy.

"In the eyes of Castro, the mob, the U.S. government and U.S. corporations were all part of the exploitation of Cuba," said T.J. English, author of *Havana Nocturne: How the Mob Owned Cuba...and Then Lost It to the Revolution.* "The dream was that Havana would be a party that never ended. Instead, it turned out to be one of the greatest hangovers of all time," he wrote in *Smithsonian* magazine.

Cuba was two separate nations. One was filled with prosperity, glamour, glitz and wealth. The other Cuba was a place where sugarcane cutters worked only four months a year, leaving them and their families in debt, hungry and malnourished. The cash investment by American business never made it to where it was needed. Cuba was beset by social problems, a high infant mortality rate, substandard housing and illiteracy among its poorest citizens.

Castro launched guerrilla war against Batista on July 26, 1953, attacking an army barracks at Moncada in what became known as the 26th of July Movement. Castro's ragtag army fought its way from its stronghold in the Sierra Maestra Mountains in southeastern Cuba to Havana, where Batista fled on New Year's Day 1959.

Batista and the Mafia were made for each other. Batista weakened labor unions, which allowed the mobsters to import their own people to run the casinos, and they began investing in real estate. Batista granted gaming licenses to anyone who invested $1 million in hotels or $200,000 in a nightclub.

Rothman was the Mannarinos' man in Havana and oversaw gambling at the Sans Souci. He was a husky, dark-haired man with green eyes who had

Sans Souci nightclub outside Havana where the Mannarino brothers ran the gambling concession. *Wikipedia*.

been around gangsters all his life. He was a bookmaker, a gambler and an ex-convict who had managed the Sans Souci in Havana for the Mannarinos in the 1950s. Rothman was born in the Bronx after his parents emigrated from Romania. In a 1961 memo from the special agent in charge of the Pittsburgh field office to J. Edgar Hoover, the agent reported that Rothman, "like all other Mannarino employees, stole from them," and noted that Rothman's "Cuban connections are overrated."

Rothman was married and had two sons. He divorced his wife and marred Olga Chaviano, an Argentine dancer who performed at the Sans Souci, and had a son with her. One of his sons became a noted fertility specialist. Dr. Cappy Rothman grew up in South Florida and enjoyed the sway his father held with racketeers.

"Everything was comped. They all knew my father. In Cuba people would call him 'Mr. Normie' walking down the street," said Rothman in an interview with the *Los Angeles Daily News*. He had front-row seats at shows at Miami's Fontainebleau Hotel to see Frank Sinatra, Sammy Davis Jr. and Dean Martin perform.

Dr. Rothman knew his father was a mobster but never pressed him about his life in the rackets until he was on his deathbed, but the senior Rothman wouldn't talk. "I never talked when I was alive. I'm certainly not going to talk when I'm dying."

He worked for Santo Trafficante Jr. after Trafficante bought out the Mannarinos. Rothman bragged to the FBI that he was "a very close personal friend of Fulgencio Batista and one of the few persons trusted by the dictator," but he also claimed to have an "acquaintanceship with Castro," according to a memo from the special agent in charge of the Miami office to J. Edgar Hoover in 1960.

"Mannarino began watching the activities of Fidel Castro and his 26th of July Movement with a view of gaining favor with him in the event the Rebellion was successful," according to Jonathan Marshall in the *Journal of Global South Studies*. Mannarino's interest in Castro was spurred by Rothman, who convinced Mannarino that Castro might be disposed to reward Mannarino with the rights to gambling if Castro deposed Batista, but Castro would need guns that the Mafia could supply.

Mannarino was drooling over the money that he believed he could make by running guns. Mannarino traveled to Camaguey, Cuba, in February to meet Rothman to discuss ways of smuggling guns to Castro. Sam told an FBI informant he "had influence with Dictator Batista as well as [the] rebel leader, Fidel Castro," according to a memo sent by the special agent in charge of Miami to Hoover on March 21. Mannarino was hardly an expert in Cuban politics but he decided to back Castro "with a view toward gaining favor with [Castro] in the event the rebellion was successful," Special Agent Richard Gordon Douce reported on July 31, 1959.

Chuck Teemer, a longtime gambler from Pittsburgh who also had a financial interest in the Sans Souci, was privy to the relationship between Sam Mannarino and Batista. Teemer told the agents who interviewed him that the Mannarinos "have been very friendly with General Batista," the special agent in charge of Pittsburgh informed Hoover in a 1958 memo titled "Gambling Activities in Cuba."

Teemer had long been associated with the Pittsburgh rackets. He began his career as a gambler in the mid-1920s, booking numbers at a McKeesport poolroom. He managed the 207 Club in Homestead, considered "the most lawless town in western Pennsylvania," according to the *Pittsburgh Post-Gazette*. Teemer also represented Mannarino interests in a series of gambling clubs along Route 30 in Hancock County, West Virginia, known as "the strip." Teemer told the FBI the Mannarinos were behind Club 30, one of the more lucrative clubs, according to a 1958 report by Special Agent Damon W. Pitcher.

With their plans in place, Mannarino and Rothman were ready to put their plan into action.

8

THE BREAK-IN

FBI special agent Harold Weida arrived at the National Guard Armory in Canton, Ohio, on the morning of October 14, 1958, and learned from city police officers that 318 weapons had vanished without a trace from storage lockers. There was no sign that the burglars had jimmied the locks on the front door or forced it open. They simply walked inside, made their way to the storage room, used bolt cutters to break the locks and then snapped the latches on the gun racks. The tally included 141 M-1 rifles, 164 carbines, 4 machine guns, 8 .22-caliber rifles and a .50-caliber machine gun. The weapons were hauled out of the south side of the building and dumped into a waiting vehicle, leaving nothing but tire impressions in the grass.

Weida suspected the heist was an inside job. Sam Mannarino, the supposed mastermind of the scheme, discussed the break-in with an FBI agent during the investigation and mused that someone had probably left the front door unlocked. "You leave the door open at an armory today and I will take the guns out," said a smiling Mannarino to Special Agent Thomas Forsyth III in a 1962 interview.

Mannarino had criminal connections in the Canton area, and the FBI learned from informants that brothers Francis and Charles LaCamera were approached by John and Phil Scardina, who controlled the rackets in Mercer County, Pennsylvania, to see if they were interested in the job. They declined. Then the Scardinas sought out two well-known professional burglars who refused the offer but suggested the Scardinas ask Youngstown

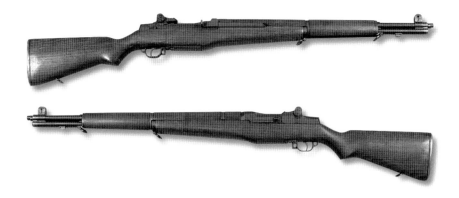

An M-1 rifle, the model stolen from a National Guard Armory in Canton, Ohio, that was bound for Fidel Castro in Cuba. *Wikipedia.*

racketeer Sandy Naples, who was affiliated with the LaRocca family in Pittsburgh if he could recommend someone.

The Canton Police immediately identified two suspects: George Florea and Philip Mainer. Florea was a safecracker and was convicted of breaking into a Fairmont, West Virginia supermarket in 1959. After his arrest, federal prosecutors told Florea they would drop the charge if he cooperated with the FBI in the armory investigation. At first, Florea agreed to meet with FBI agents but changed his mind, claiming he knew nothing about the burglary.

The FBI focused on Florea because he knew Sam Mannarino. Agents tracked a series of phone calls between Florea and Mannarino that made them suspicious. When agents questioned Florea, he denied any involvement in the theft, claiming he "would not be involved in such a thing." Florea also denied knowing Mannarino. As far as the telephone calls, Florea denied making them and said, "Maybe somebody called the wrong number." FBI suspicions grew after discovering telephone calls were made from Mannarino's private office number in New Kensington to Dominick Dellerba, Florea's brother-in-law in Ohio, which increased their suspicion that the Mafia likely was involved.

Weida learned from an informant that Mainer had sold Kelly Mannarino 1,800 cartons of stolen cigarettes for a dollar a carton, so he knew that Mainer was acquainted with the Mannarinos and the New Kensington area and likely was a source of contact.

"Sufficient proof has been uncovered to positively connect Mannarino with the theft, but because of his high position among hoodlum elements in the Pittsburgh area, witnesses who are willing to testify against him are almost nonexistent," wrote Hoover to the Pittsburgh, Cleveland and Miami field offices on December 21, 1959. "Therefore, insufficient evidence has been accumulated to sustain a successful prosecution."

The Canton burglary was one of several at armories across the United States in 1958 that bore similarities to the Canton break-in. Agents were trying to trace a cache of weapons stolen in North Carolina and in Waco, Texas, that they believed were destined for Cuba.

Canton is in the middle of Stark County and is the hometown of President William McKinley and the site of the National Football League Hall of Fame. It also was the home of James "Jumbo" Crowley, a notorious gangster, corruptor of police and politicians in the 1920s and 1930s. Editor Don Mellett of the *Canton Daily News* was murdered in 1926 for exposing the ties between criminals and corrupt police officials. Five people, including Canton's police chief, were arrested for the murder. The chief was acquitted but four were sentenced to life in prison. The city was dubbed "Little Chicago" because elected officials shared a cozy bed with the Mafia just like Al Capone did with Chicago officials.

The Canton-based military unit drilled the day before the burglary, and Sergeant Wilbert Shue and Master Sergeant Wayne Bigler told Weida they locked the building before leaving. Bigler said he also chained the front door after locking it before leaving the post. Chief Warrant Officer Curtis W. Blocker said he locked the supply room when he left, but he discovered the next morning that the room was unlocked. Canton Police located a stolen truck on October 21 that the owner said contained a wrench and a bolt cutter that were missing and had more miles on the odometer than the owner remembered. Found underneath the seat was a door key to a Miami motel, according to a 151-page report filed by Weida. It was the same motel where Mannarino and other conspirators had gathered to discuss ways to dispose of the guns.

Weida had no shortage of suspects. Every current and former member of the National Guard unit came under suspicion. Major Thomas Herzog, who commanded the unit, said dozens of current and former members of the National Guard had keys to the building that were never returned but only the company commanders and supply sergeants had keys to the rooms where weapons were stored. Agents combed police reports for stolen trucks and checked with car dealers for anyone who might have recently purchased a new or used vehicle. They scoured local airports to check on flights in and out of the Canton area and questioned gun store owners for anyone who had purchased large supplies of ammunition.

Then another suspect surfaced. Louis Martinez was a deadbeat lawyer in financial trouble who frequently traveled to Florida and Cuba. Martinez was viewed in Canton as a "shifty character" who left a trail of debt and unpaid loans but who also had connections to pro-Castro Cubans in New York. Martinez and Florea knew each other because they grew up together in the same Canton neighborhood. Weida became intrigued after learning that Martinez also knew Mannarino's friend Joseph Merola, who vouched for Martinez with the authorities in Havana after Martinez was jailed for failing to pay his hotel bill and then released.

Martinez was a nomad. He had no fixed address and traveled often but refused to tell the FBI where he derived his income when FBI agents questioned him. He portrayed himself as an adventurer and carried a .38-caliber pistol in a shoulder holster. Martinez's family considered him a "black sheep." He suffered a stroke when he was two years old that left him with a partially paralyzed left hand and arm. He graduated from law school at Ohio State University but never practiced much law.

"Louis is always talking about the fact that he is going to make a lot of money, but he has never made any money to my knowledge and owes everybody in town," said his brother John. Sally Krajcik, a former girlfriend, told the FBI that Martinez admitted to her that he had been buying guns for Castro and that Martinez purchased eight drums of napalm, an explosive jelly-like substance, shipped to South America for eventual transport to Cuban rebels, according to Special Agent Samuel Farrin, who interviewed Krajcik.

There were rumors in Canton within the city's Hispanic community that Martinez worked for Castro and expected to be "riding the gravy train" after Batista was deposed. The *Canton Times* published a series of articles on the Cuban revolution beginning on March 27, 1959. One story featured a photograph of Martinez seated next to Castro. The caption beneath the picture read, "Fidel Castro…is shown here with his friend, local attorney Louis Martinez, who arranged an interview with Castro and the various newsmen who were anxious to meet the Cuban hero." Despite an extensive probe, Martinez was never charged with any crimes related to the break-in.

The FBI then shifted its focus to Joseph Merola of Pittsburgh after learning from the Bureau of Alcohol Tobacco and Firearms that Merola was in New York trying to buy guns for Castro. An ATF informant, Arnold

Rayber, was provided several guns by ATF agents to show Merola, who boasted that he smuggled more than $1 million worth of guns into Cuba and that his underworld associates expected "fat gambling concessions from the new government" once Fulgencio Batista was deposed. After inspecting Rayber's guns, an elated Merola said, "This is what I want, get me all you can but clean them up," according to a 1959 FBI report sent to Hoover.

Rayber was contacted by Charles Colle, a gun dealer from Union, New Jersey, who said he had access to a supply of M-1 rifles that were stolen from an armory in Ohio and the seller wanted sixty dollars per gun. Colle would have to meet the seller in Washington, D.C., and from there, they would travel to where the guns were stored. The FBI suspected the seller was Sam Mannarino after agents confirmed that Mannarino was in the capital in late October 1958 and had flown to Miami on October 24, where he registered at the Sea Gull Motel as "Sal Mann." The motel matched the key found beneath the seat in the abandoned truck.

JOSEPH MEROLA
Denies charges.

Joseph Merola was an FBI informant who provided the FBI with information on the criminal activities of the Mannarino brothers. *American Mafia History.*

Merola managed the Garden of Allah Motel in Miami, a hangout for mobsters, and the FBI suspected Merola used the business to store stolen weapons. Motel janitor Frank Frazier told FBI agent George Davis Jr. that Merola kept heavy wooden crates at the motel that were secured by metal bands along with surplus U.S. military uniforms and boots. His wife, Nellie, who worked as a maid, was present when Merola opened one of the crates and said she saw rifles inside. The special agent in charge of the Miami field office notified Hoover on December 29, 1959, about the interviews, which led the bureau to focus hard on Merola.

Customs agents informed the FBI that it had tracked a boat named *Menace* that Merola claimed to own that had carried several Cubans and a shipment of weapons destined for Cuba. The voyage was abandoned because of engine trouble. Hans Milton, an experienced boat captain and mechanic, was hired by Merola to inspect the vessel and told Merola the engine badly needed an overhaul but Merola dismissed his assessment and set off for Key West on what Merola claimed was a fishing trip.

Milton was suspicious of Merola's story after he saw the *Menace* was stocked with a large supply of food and large, heavy suitcases, which Milton suspected contained guns. The vessel ran aground in Key West, and when customs agents boarded the boat, the guns and Cubans were missing but a large supply of food and cans filled with gasoline were onboard. The supplies would have been sufficient for the vessel to reach Cuba, according to a September 22, 1959 interview of Milton by FBI agent George E. Davis Jr.

A check of Merola's telephone records revealed that he made a series of calls from Miami to New Kensington, Havana and New York City, which the FBI suspected was connected to the plan to ship the stolen military weapons to Cuba. One of the calls Merola made was to Victor Carlucci, Sam Mannarino's son-in-law in New Kensington, who was suspected of storing the stolen weapons at his beer distributorship before they were transported to the Remich Airport.

Merola also was acquainted with Rothman, who managed the Biltmore Terrace Hotel, a hangout for Cuban exiles longing for the days before Castro came to power. The hotel was a gathering place for displaced Cubans who dreamed of returning to the island and deposing Castro. With Rothman's connections to Sam Mannarino and organized crime, the Mafia was a likely source to obtain guns.

Rothman seemed ambivalent about Castro. On the one hand, he tried to supply him with guns. On the other hand, he tried to topple him after Castro assumed power. The FBI learned in late 1959 that Rothman had traveled to Yucatan in southeastern Mexico to establish a base of operations against Castro along with Roberto Fernandez Miranda, Batista's brother-in-law; Eduardo "Teddy" Whitehouse, a former official with the Cuban Aeronautical Association; and former army colonel Orlando Negueruela, according to classified CIA memo in 1961.

Rothman hired Chicago attorney Luis Kutner to approach the U.S. Department of Justice offering Rothman's aid in eliminating Castro. On May 26, 1960, Assistant U.S. Attorney James B. Parsons wrote a memo detailing his meeting with Kutner:

> *Rothman has been a close personal friend of Fulgencio Batista and is one of the few persons trusted by Batista....In fact he, Rothman, during the time Batista was in power, was in charge of all gambling in Cuba.*

Having known Batista as well as he claims and being aware of his current activities and also revolutionary activities, he is in a position to known what may happen in Cuba in the future. As a matter of fact, he claims to be able to deliver Castro to be wiped out. Rothman likewise claims an acquaintanceship with Castro.

The FBI wanted Kutner to "determine what information Norman Rothman might have which might be of interest to the Bureau or any other Government agency." The Church Committee, during its 1975 investigation into joint efforts by the CIA and Mafia to kill Castro, determined the plot was first discussed in August 1960, a few months after Rothman made the offer to the U.S. government, and placed him at the center of the conspiracy. Rothman had met with CIA agents who then discussed the scheme with Mafia associates that included Santo Trafficante Jr. and Sam Mannarino but turned the task over to Johnny Roselli. Roselli testified before the Church Committee in 1975 and was scheduled to appear a second time, but he could not be found. He was murdered, and his body was found on August 7, 1976, stuffed inside an oil drum near Miami.

After Rothman was convicted of gun smuggling, he tried to convince the government to help him with his pending prison sentence by offering to kill Castro. Rothman claimed to have assets in Cuba and the Caribbean, and White House and CIA officials wanted to meet with him to assess his "operational potential." Rothman refused to identify the names of his operatives to agency officials. The CIA suspected Rothman was all talk. "I do not believe it is in the interests of the U.S. government to further discuss with Mr. Rothman these particular claims," according to a memorandum to the Deputy CIA station chief on June 29, 1961.

Rothman claimed the Kennedy administration tried to recruit him to help kill Castro. He said he met with Harry Hall Wilson, a White House lawyer, and John Seigenthaler, an assistant U.S. attorney general. "One of them happened to discuss [the assassination of Castro] with me but not in a technical way. You know, just in a casual way. That was about it. I cannot for the moment remember it word for word because it was far back," said Rothman. He told FBI agents that if the United States "would give him a free hand he could arrange for Castro's assassination. He added he was not even interested in being paid for his services in this regard," according to a report by the House Select Committee on Assassinations.

In exchange for his help, Rothman wanted government aid with his pending five-year prison term for his gunrunning conviction. "Rothman frankly stated he could not perform such services…if he were serving time in jail," read an FBI report. He told officials he could "deliver Castro" to the United States and arrange for Castro to be "wiped out." Rothman told FBI agents Edward Kinzer and Robert Malone that he tried to recruit Frank Sturgis, also known as Frank Fiorini, to kill Castro, but Sturgis denied the claim.

Meanwhile, investigators continued receiving anonymous tips about the whereabout of the stolen guns, which proved little help. Canton police chief J.B. Quilligan received an anonymous letter postmarked from Pittsburgh on November 9, 1959, that contained a detailed sketch of a barn in Butler County, Pennsylvania, claiming the stolen guns were stored there. The barn was located seven miles from the Allegheny Valley Airport, operated by Tony Remich. There was "a light burning inside" the building read the note, which described the layout of the barn and said the letter's author had seen "trucks loading and unloading" at the site, but the FBI found an innocent explanation. The barn's owner was running a business from his home and used the barn as a warehouse.

While the FBI was tracking the stolen weapons, the border patrol and customs agents were trying to locate four twin-engine Beechcraft airplanes suspected of ferrying weapons to Cuba. One aircraft drew their attention. The plane's tail number had been found in the wreckage of another plane that had crashed in Guantanamo Bay, Cuba, filled with contraband guns destined for Cuba.

The plane with the tail number N-76165C was on a watch list sent to airports along the East Coast when air traffic controllers near Pittsburgh alerted authorities that the plane had just landed at the Allegheny County Airport. Border patrol agent Peter Grootendorst was notified and immediately headed to Pittsburgh.

9

WHEELS UP

Grootendorst arrived at the Allegheny Valley Airport just as the twin-engine Beechcraft was hurtling down the runway for takeoff. Minutes earlier, Pennsylvania state trooper Cornelius Coyle had seen a truck bearing the logo of S&S Vending Company of New Kensington pull up to the aircraft and watched several men removing items from the truck covered in burlap and loading them onto the plane.

Grootendorst, who was born in the Netherlands and immigrated to the United States in 1946, had inspected the interior of the plane the night before it landed at the Allegheny County Airport in West Mifflin to make sure it was empty. The next morning, pilot Stuart Sutor took off at 9:00 a.m. and turned north, flying over Pittsburgh near the KDKA-TV broadcast antenna. Then he made a right turn and steered east before circling and landing at the Remich airstrip a half hour later. An air traffic controller asked the pilot of a passing Allegheny Airlines passenger jet to alter his flight path over Remich to confirm the Beechcraft was on the ground.

Telephone records indicated that someone—likely Joseph Merola—made a telephone call from Remich to Victor Carlucci, Sam Mannarino's son-in-law. Fifteen minutes later, Daniel "Speedo" Hanna arrived in the truck loaded with guns.

Troopers were about to seize the aircraft, but Sutor took off before they could move in. The plane turned south headed for Morgantown, which was sixty-seven miles away. Grootendorst immediately commandeered a private plane to pursue the aircraft and alerted the West Virginia State Police.

The Remich Airport was owned by Anthony Remich and catered to recreational pilots, but the landing of the large Beechcraft with the green-and-white paint job attracted the attention of nearby residents. Next to the strip was a U.S. Army Nike Missile Battery, one of a series of missile sites that ringed Pittsburgh during the Cold War.

Sutor was also on a U.S. Border Patrol watch list of pilots suspected of helping supply Castro with arms. Pilots in South Florida were in demand, receiving hundreds of dollars per trip to fly weapons from Florida to rural airstrips in Cuba, where Castro's guerrillas were waiting to unload the cargo. Sutor landed in Morgantown and taxied up to the gas pumps and purchased 147 gallons of aviation fuel. He gave airport manager Lee Rinick a one-hundred-dollar bill to pay for the gas, but Rinick was alerted to Sutor's arrival and stalled for time by fumbling for change to give West Virginia State Police time to arrive.

Sutor was preparing to take off just as a state trooper and Monongalia County deputy sheriffs arrived and detained him. Grootendorst landed a short time later, searched the aircraft and found 123 stolen weapons stacked three feet high in the fuselage. These were the arms stolen from the National Guard Armory in Canton, Ohio, in October.

Inside were ninety-two M-1 rifles, twenty-four carbines, four submachine guns, a .22-caliber rifle and two dismantled .50-caliber machine guns. Investigators also found a tag inside the fuselage that bore the handwritten words "Btry A, 182d AAA Bn," which indicated the armaments came from the antiaircraft artillery battalion Battery A of the Ohio National Guard. The guns were wrapped in thirty-six burlap bags and tied with twine. The FBI traced the bags to a feed store in the New Kensington area with the brand names "Wayne Hog Balancer" and "Gold Medal Mash" along with peanuts, oats and wheat grains, according to FBI records.

"You can usually tell when law officers are around an airport when you arrive but I didn't have any idea anything had gone wrong," said Sutor as he stood glumly outside the plane with his hands in his pockets as two state troopers stood

Stolen weapons wrapped in burlap after they were seized by the government at an airport in West Virginia. *From the* Greensburg Tribune-Review.

behind him. The *Morgantown Post* reported that Sutor complained to police that he had flown all over the world only to be arrested "by a bunch of hillbillies," he told a reporter.

Sutor was "smug," "uncooperative" and "evasive" when FBI agents arrived in Morgantown to question him. He told Special Agent Richard Gordon Douce he was "wasting taxpayers' money" by arresting him because "he might not know as much about the gunrunning operation as one might think." Grootendorst also tried to question Sutor at the Monongalia County Jail in Morgantown, but Sutor refused to answer any questions without a lawyer and claimed that he was unaware of the contents of his cargo because the items were wrapped in burlap sacks.

FBI special agent J. Edward Madvay described Sutor as a "mercenary pilot who would fly a plane for anybody, any place, for any amount of money." Sutor was slightly built with brown curly hair and blue eyes. He had been fascinated by airplanes ever since he was a teenager in the late 1930s loafing at a local airport in St. Petersburg, Florida.

He worked as a pilot in Scotland for Trans World Airlines after World War II, for Inter-American Airways in 1948 and then for Ransa Airlines in Miami ferrying B-26 bombers from India to the United States. In 1958, he was working for Western Hemisphere Export in Miami before he started his own business buying old aircraft, refitting them and selling them.

Sutor was arraigned before a U.S. magistrate in Fairmont, West Virginia, and held in the Marion County Jail. He complained about the "ridiculously high bond" of $20,000 that prevented his release and suspected the FBI had him confined in a small cell with "degenerates" to force him to cooperate. He wanted to be released on bond "in the worst way" because he feared his wife in Florida would "tell everything to the FBI if enough pressure was brought to bear on her," added Madvay. Sutor was also scared. He knew that if she blabbed about his mob connections, he was a dead man.

Sutor had a great deal to hide from the FBI. He was no stranger to the Caribbean. The CIA notified the FBI that a pilot, believed to be Sutor, had been in Guatemala buying forty tons of Italian-made weapons for Castro. Attorney Richard Bergstresser of Florida telephoned Sutor at the Marion County Jail in Fairmont, West Virginia, where he had been transferred and warned him not to say anything to the FBI. A deputy U.S. marshal monitoring the call reported that Bergstresser advised Sutor, "Whatever you do, don't make any statements until promised complete immunity."

Sutor knew the people he was working for were connected to the Mafia, but U.S. Attorney Hubert Teitelbaum offered to drop the charges against him if he would testify for the federal government and implicate his employers. Sutor refused to cooperate. Miami attorney Max Lurie told Sutor to invoke the Fifth Amendment if he was called to testify before a federal grand jury. The FBI obtained Lurie's telephone records and discovered he had been in contact with Sam Mannarino, who likely relayed a threat to Sutor via Lurie to keep his mouth shut.

An anxious Sutor warned Lurie that he could keep quiet for only so long. "I'd rather be outside fighting any kind of fight too—any kind of fight—do you understand what I mean? Any kind of fight. You better understand what I mean." Sutor's hopes for release were shattered when Bergstresser told him he was on his own. "The interested parties have abandoned you, they want nothing to do with you."

Authorities thought they had found another stolen shipment of guns in 1962 when scuba divers located ninety-seven rifles, shotguns, pistols and submachine guns in the Cheat River outside Morgantown in an area known as Criminal Cove. Authorities initially suspected the guns were a shipment destined for Cuba that had been ditched in the water, but an investigation revealed they belonged to a coal company, which received the weapons during World War II under the Civilian Defense Authority, according to the *Dominion News*.

The special agent in charge of the Pittsburgh field office notified FBI headquarters that there was a "remote possibility" that the twin-engine Beechcraft piloted by Sutor may have also been used to fly weapons stolen from a National Guard Armory in Newton, North Carolina. Thieves had removed six Browning automatic rifles, forty M-1 carbines, a .30-caliber machine gun, fourteen .30-caliber carbines and eleven .45-caliber handguns. The plane's registered owner was DuPont Air Interests in Miami Springs, Florida, the same firm Sutor had leased his plane from.

Sutor's Beechcraft was tracked on several suspicious flights around the Caribbean and Central America. It had been flown from Miami to Jamaica and to Venezuela and Colombia before returning to Miami. Then the aircraft traveled to the Grand Caymans and Costa Rica. The plane was built for the U.S. Army Air Corp and sold as surplus in 1957 to Charles Hormel for one dollar. Hormel was described in newspaper accounts as a "soldier of fortune" and had been arrested on gunrunning charges in Jamaica two weeks before he was nabbed with a carload of military-grade weapons that included two .50-caliber machine guns, sixty-five rifles and fifteen thousand rounds of ammunition destined for Cuban rebels.

Hormel told the *Miami Herald* he flew to Cuba four times a week, and on one trip, he was forced to ditch the Aero Commander he was piloting after the craft ran out of gas, requiring him to bail out in Guantanamo Bay, Cuba. He was ferrying twenty-five submachine guns and sixteen thousand rounds of ammunition. Hormel was rescued by the U.S. Navy, and the plane was salvaged. Found in the wreckage was a flight log indicating that Hormel had flown the same Beechcraft that Sutor piloted on thirty-six separate flights, earning the plane a spot on a Border Patrol watch list.

Florida was ground zero for international intrigue in the late 1950s. Castro's agents undertook clandestine efforts to purchase weapons on the black market for shipment to Cuba. They purchased weapons from gun stores throughout the state and then hid them in the homes of sympathizers until they could be smuggled into Cuba, according to Ricardo Lorie y Valla, Castro's former chief arms buyer, who testified before the Senate Internal Security Subcommittee in 1964 after breaking with Castro. Storing the weapons until they could be moved to Cuba was dangerous. Phosphorous bombs exploded in an apartment building in Miami owned by a Castro supporter. Police later found one hundred homemade bombs and three thousand rounds of ammo hidden in several apartments. Detectives found nine hundred sticks of dynamite and two submachine guns hidden in a Miami Beach hotel.

The Border Patrol was stretched thin monitoring the southern Florida coastline's miles of mangrove swamps, inlets and fishing shacks that pro-Castro Cubans used to store guns. There also were over two hundred airfields and airstrips in the region where planes could take off and land on their trips unobserved. The border patrol reported seizing $200,000 worth of arms in 1959—only a fraction of the weapons that made it to Cuba, according to an FBI report titled *Foreign Political Matters Cuba in 1960*.

Customs agents said the flow of weapons through Florida to Cuba was a continuing operation. Border patrol agents boarded a yacht in Key Biscayne filled with two hundred rifles and seven thousand rounds of ammunition. In another case in 1959, the agency seized an airplane in Key Largo bound for Cuba loaded with fifteen rifles and twenty thousand rounds of ammunition. Some of the guns had been issued to prison officers and security guards employed by the Atomic Energy Commission at nuclear power plants, according to the FBI.

In 1959, three Cubans were arrested on the Florida Turnpike with two hundred M-1 rifles. That same year, eight men were arrested on a yacht carrying two hundred rifles and two thousand rounds of ammunition. Two more Cubans were arrested the following month with thirty rifles and twenty thousand rounds as they tried to take off for Pinar del Rio province in Cuba. "The guns come from all over the United States," said a customs agent. Police arrested five men with a truckload of guns at Miami International Airport in 1959, and ten men were arrested while loading twenty thousand rounds of ammunition onto a C-47 aircraft. Miami was fast becoming the "Casablanca of the Caribbean" because of the influx of gun smugglers, pro and anti-Castro forces, political exiles, spies and tourists, reported the *Miami Herald*.

The U.S. government was reluctant to prosecute the Cuban smugglers for fear that many of them might turn out to be future leaders in a post-Batista government. After customs agents arrested 150 Cubans in 1959 for violating the Neutrality Act, they were freed on bond and fled to Cuba. Government prosecutors hinted they would take a lenient view of punishment if they voluntarily returned to Florida to answer the charges.

Airplane owners reaped financial rewards by renting or leasing their planes for short-term charters along with bush pilots who were paid hefty fees to fly planeloads of guns and ammunition into Cuba's mountains and rural areas. It was common knowledge among pilots that they could earn substantial money flying weapons to clandestine air strips in Cuba, reported the *Miami Herald* in 1959.

One flight that was intercepted by customs agents revealed a shipment of shotguns, M-1 carbines, ammunition and .45-caliber pistols with the words "National Guard" imprinted on the butts. The pilot told agents he was paid $900 to fly a load of shotguns, rifles, pistols and ammunition to rebels who would meet the plane when it landed. He flew another shipment to the outskirts of Havana in July and August 1959 and was paid another $900.

Customs agents seized two yachts bound for Cuba containing a total of sixty-two Cuban nationals, thousands of dollars' worth of weapons, medical supplies and military gear. An aging B-18 bomber was seized before taking off at a South Florida airstrip filled with guns and carrying twenty-two Cuban rebels. Inside the fuselage were packages of weapons and ammunition marked with the name "Fidel." Castro agents also used attractive young women with small arms stashed in their carry-on luggage to board planes bound for Cuba. In 1958, Jesus Yanez Pelletier, a Cuban agent, spent $100,000 buying guns, reported the *New York Times*.

Smuggling guns had been going on since Spain controlled the island. Napoleon Broward was a steamboat captain and politician who would become Florida's governor. In the 1890s, he made eight trips from Florida to Cuba to arm rebels trying to overthrow Spanish rule. "Gun running is an ancient art in Central and South America, well-practiced and well-understood in many quarters," according to a CIA report.

10

THE INVESTIGATION

FBI special agent Richard Gordon Douce was suspicious of Anthony Remich, the operator of the Allegheny Valley Airport. There were too many coincidences to suit Douce. Even though Remich denied that he was involved in the gunrunning scheme, Douce remained skeptical. First, Remich lived in New Kensington and was Kelly Mannarinio's neighbor. Second, Kelly Mannarino was godfather to one of Remich's sons. Third, Remich had been an invited guest to the wedding of Kelly Mannarino's daughter. Finally, Remich was born in Italy, and his last name was "Remicci," according to genealogy records—although FBI reports list the spelling as "Remmigi" before he legally changed it to Remich.

There were other aspects of the probe that bothered Douce. Remich taught a key witness in the investigation, Dr. Louis Pessolano, how to fly. Pessolano was a native of New Kensington before he moved to Florida and leased the Beechcraft that Stuart Sutor flew. Pessolano grew up with the Mannarinos and was asked by Norman Rothman to lease a plane and hire a pilot for the job. Finally, the plotters selected Remich's airstrip to fly the guns south. Despite Douce's misgivings, Remich was never charged with any crime. Remich also knew Daniel "Speedo" Hanna, Joseph "Red" Giordano and Joseph Merola, a gunrunner and jewel thief who had grown close to the Mannarino brothers.

What really heightened Douce's suspicion about Remich was learning that the November flight was not Sutor's first flight from the airport. Remich revealed to Douce that Sutor had landed there the month before and identified Carlucci, Sutor, Hanna and Merola as being present that day. "Investigation reflects that Sutor hauled one load of guns from the Pittsburgh area to Miami, Florida," read Agent Douce's report.

After Sutor took off on October 26, he was forced to land at the Washington County Airport, south of Pittsburgh, because of bad weather before resuming his flight to Morgantown, West Virginia, and then onto Savannah, Georgia, where Agents George Davis Jr. and Leman J. Stafford Jr. informed the Miami field office that first shipment of guns was either transferred to Cuban rebels who shipped the weapons to Cuba by boat or flown directly to Cuba.

John Remich, son of the owner, was at the strip on October 26 when the same Beechcraft landed. He saw Carlucci arrive in his red Oldsmobile containing Merola and then saw a truck with the logo of S&S Vending Company arrive and park near the plane. Douce interviewed John Remich on November 20.

Douce wondered if the weapons were from the National Guard Army in Canton or from some other source. On the morning of the November flight, Carlucci told the FBI that he was voting in New Kensington because it was Election Day and said a nun from a New Kensington parochial school was standing in line and would support his alibi. Mother Superior Pauline Simons was standing in line to vote that morning along with Sisters Ann Martin, Karin Schnoss, Margaret Mancinskas and Mary Philomona, according to Westmoreland County voting records reviewed by agents, but Simons said she couldn't remember seeing Carlucci, whom she barely knew. Agents placed Carlucci and his two vehicles, an English Prefect and an Oldsmobile, at the airport that morning through eyewitness testimony at the time he claimed to be voting.

Howard McGraw, who lived near the airstrip, identified Sutor and Carlucci standing together. Joseph Drag, who was working on the roof of his house overlooking the airport, said he watched the men load the plane with cargo that was stored in the truck. Pennsylvania state trooper Cornelius Coyle had the plane under surveillance and saw men taking items from the truck and placing them on the aircraft just before takeoff.

The origin of the gunrunning plot began with a telephone conversation between Norman Rothman and Dr. Louis Pessolano, who lied to the FBI when he claimed he leased a plane for a man calling from Pennsylvania who wanted to take friends on a hunting and fishing trip in Florida. Rothman also wanted Pessolano to hire a pilot who could keep his mouth shut. Since Pessolano was a pilot and worked as a physician for the Civil Aeronautics

Board, Mannarino and Rothman believed he had the contacts to hire the right man for the mission.

Special Agents Richard Gordon Douce and Thomas Forsyth III knew Pessolano was lying when he was questioned in Florida on January 15, 1959. Pessolano was subpoenaed to appear before a federal grand jury and lied under oath when he testified that Sam Mannarino was not involved in the plot. Douce and Forsyth wanted Pessolano to return to Pittsburgh for further questioning, but the physician begged off, claiming he was too busy with his medical practice. The truth was that Pessolano had a gambling problem and was broke.

The agents got him to return north by paying his travel expenses. Pessolano relented and told agents that Mannarino called him about hiring Sutor. He lied before the grand jury because he feared Mannarino would kill him if Pessolano implicated his childhood friend in the conspiracy. He also lied because he wanted to shield Sutor. "I felt a sense of obligation to the young man because of my having involved him in this situation and further knowing his economic distress." Despite his admitted perjury, Pessolano was not charged with any crime but was named as an unindicted coconspirator.

"The call that came from Rothman I believe was local in nature and not long distance and it was probably made from his home in Surfside, Fla.," said Pessalano in a statement he gave to FBI agents on October 16, 1958. "There was no mention of money during the first call but there was a request for a pilot."

Pessolano had difficulty finding a qualified pilot. He offered Charles "Pete" Smith the job, but Smith begged off because the plane was in poor condition. "This is a junker. I wouldn't fly it," Smith told Pessolano. Smith said the plane also needed a better radio in case the pilot ran into trouble during the flight, according to an account in the *Pittsburgh Press.*

In a desperate effort to find a pilot, Joseph Merola kidnapped Fausto Gomez, a former Cuban Air Force pilot who defected and was living in Florida and tried to force him at gunpoint to take the job. Gomez refused and was eventually released.

Pessolano remained in contact with Rothman, who was shuttling between Florida and Havana, and told him he had hired Sutor. Rothman wanted to know if Sutor was the "right guy," a man who was a capable pilot but also would keep his mouth shut. Pessolano vouched for Sutor, so Rothman gave the doctor $6,000 in $100 bills wrapped in a newspaper to pay to lease the aircraft on October 16, 1958. Sutor was no stranger to Caribbean intrigue and asked Rothman directly whether the cargo was guns. "It is guns," Rothman told him. "I asked Sutor if he knew the nature of the cargo and he answered they were guns," said Pessolano in his statement to the FBI.

After the conspirators were arrested, a frantic Sam Mannarino called Pessolano. "Doc, have you heard what happened? They picked up Vic [Carlucci]. I was astonished to hear it and so stated to Sam," Pessolano told FBI agents.

Pessolano grew up in New Kensington with the Mannarinos. He was captain of the 1928 undefeated Villanova football team and then played briefly in the NFL for the Staten Island Stapletons. After finishing medical school, he became a professional wrestler before serving as a captain in the U.S. Public Health Service and practiced medicine in New Kensington before moving to Florida.

Although he escaped prosecution for gunrunning, Pessolano couldn't avoid prison. He went to prison in 1964 after being convicted of performing an illegal abortion on a sixteen-year-old girl, according to Florida court records.

FBI agents in Pittsburgh were frustrated by the lack of direct testimony linking Mannarino to the weapons. "Although the Federal Government is unable to prove it, there is no question that Samuel Mannarino was part of the conspiracy," wrote the special agent in charge of the Pittsburgh office.

11

O CANADA

Courthouse Avenue in Brockville, Ontario, was quiet on the early spring evening of May 3, 1958. Light from the moon bathed a war memorial while the lights burned brightly at the Brockville Club, a watering hole for local businessmen. The city along the shores of Lake Ontario faces the Saint Lawrence River across from Morristown, New York, and is known as the "City of the 1000 Islands." Brockville was founded by William Buell of Connecticut, who fought on the side of the British during the American Revolution and fled to Canada after war.

Rene Martin sat at a table at a roadside café on the eastern end of the city waiting for three companions who were about to pull off the largest bank heist in the history of Canada at the time. Rene Robert, Peter "The Russian" Stepanoff and Kenneth "China Boy" Winford arrived, and Martin joined them.

The robbery was well planned. The thieves knew when and how to enter the bank unnoticed. They calculated the exact spot to drill through the floors to gain access to the vault room and how to penetrate the vault. They opened only 36 of the 190 safe deposit boxes—containing $2.2 million in negotiable securities—because the doors were marked in lipstick by an inside man who was described as a quiet, well-dressed businessman who rented a safe deposit box at Brockville. Police suspect that man was William Rabin, who had made frequent trips to case the building's layout and the vault room, according to the *Winnipeg Tribune*.

Brockville at night. *Wikimedia.*

Martin was a member of a Canadian Mafia family led by brothers Vincenzo "The Egg" and Giuseppe "Pep" Cotroni. Rene Robert was Pep Cotroni's right-hand man. Police suspected Stepanoff planned the heist, and Kenneth "China Boy" Winford was an expert in explosives. The Cotronis led one of Montreal's Mafia families and were the largest heroin distributors in North America. Pep Cotroni was born in Italy but was raised in Montreal's "Little Italy" neighborhood. He attended the summit meeting of top mobsters in Apalachin, New York, in 1957, and his family was allied with the Joseph Bonano organization in New York.

The burglars arrived at the bank. They broke into the adjacent Fulford Building, climbed the stairs and entered a real estate office on the third floor while lugging acetylene tanks, crowbars, prybars, drills, hammers, gas masks and a fan. The gang put on overalls and then entered another office and began cutting a hole twenty-eight by fourteen inches through two levels of flooring and a tin ceiling to reach the vault room. They climbed down a ladder into the vault and began cutting through two inches of brick, cement and tempered steel with acetylene torches. Police estimated the work took five hours. The cutting torches and dust from the drilling filled the room with acrid smoke, which was dissipated by the fan, according to the *Winnipeg Tribune.*

When their work was finished, the men climbed upstairs, cleaned up, changed their clothes and fled. The thieves had made off with more than $12 million in bonds, cash and jewelry, including more than $2.2 million in negotiable securities, in what the local newspaper, the *Recorder and Times*, bannered in its May 5 edition, "$2,265,000—Canada's Largest." Estimates of the haul differed in newspaper, police and court records; the figure kept growing, so no one knew exactly how much was taken. The FBI pegged the value at $3.5 million in bearer bonds, $5 million in registered securities, $15,000 in cash and $40,000 in jewelry.

When the police arrived at the bank on Monday morning, they found the vault littered with debris and burned papers, but they quickly identified one of the culprits. Rene Martin had dropped his identification inside the vault. When police arrested Martin, they found a key to a railroad storage locker in his possession that contained more than $100,000 in bonds. Police later raided an apartment maintained by Pep Cotroni and discovered more bonds and a large quantity of heroin.

Canadian police suspected the Contronis were behind a series of bond thefts plaguing Canadian financial institutions amounting to millions of dollars. More than $1.8 million was stolen from a Montreal bank in January 1958, and $837,000 was stolen from an Ontario bank in January 1959.

Hole made by burglars to reach the vault at the Brockville Bank and Trust. From the Winnipeg Tribune.

After the heist, Pep Cotroni, Rene Robert, Norman Rothman, William Rabin (a shady businessman) and Mannarino met at the Sea Gull Motel in Miami to discuss how to turn the bonds into cash. Mannarino tasked Rothman with the job of converting securities into cash and Rothman tabbed Rabin, a former business partner of Mannarino in a jukebox manufacturing business, to fly to Switzerland, where he met George Rosden, a German American lawyer. Rosden was going to help Rabin obtain the financing by using the bonds as collateral for loans to buy a bank to launder the stolen money.

Pep Cotroni, head of a Canadian Mafia crime family, who was behind the burglary of the Brockville Bank and Trust. *Canadian Police photo.*

Maclean's, a Canadian magazine in 1963, described Rabin as an "apple-cheeked, cane-carrying" former Winnipeg resident who was a sophisticated and well-educated man who favored tailored suits. He was born Wolfe Rabinovich in the rural town of Morden in Manitoba in 1907 and was a musician, engineer and inventor. He invented the Maestro, a jukebox that held thirty records, according to *Jukebox Empire: The Mob and the Dark Side of the American Dream.*

He also owned the Continental Radio Corporation and was a former business partner with Sam Mannarino in the Filben Corporation, a maker of jukeboxes and slot machines that went bust a few years earlier and cost Mannarino hundreds of thousands of dollars. Rosden was an attorney and a naturalized American citizen who immigrated to the United States from Germany and had contacts in the German banking community.

Rabin and Rosden flew to Switzerland and met with officials at Leu and Company, based in Zurich, to negotiate a $3 million loan. Then Rabin and Rosden flew to Liechtenstein and formed the Central Trust Corporation, a paper corporation, that would receive the loan, but there was a problem. Bank officials checked the numbers on the bonds to make certain the documents were legitimate, which drew objections from Rabin. He claimed he had made millions of dollars during World War II that he invested in Canadian bonds but never paid taxes on the windfall.

Leu and Company officials noticed that the edges of the bonds were singed, likely from the flame of the cutting torches, and checked the numbers on the securities, only to discover they were stolen from a Canadian bank. Swiss authorities contacted the FBI and the Royal Canadian Mounted Police, according to the *Chicago Daily Tribune*.

The investigation grew more complicated when the FBI arrested Edward Browder Jr., a self-described soldier of fortune and Rothman associate who was trying to peddle a portion of the bonds. FBI reports described Browder as a "facile liar," a "highly publicized man of intrigue on Latin America revolutionaries" and an "unscrupulous adventurer who is willing to sell his services to the highest bidder."

Browder was born in Texas and had a lengthy criminal record. He was arrested in 1947 for stealing guns from an army base in Georgia and for involvement in an attempted coup against President Rómulo Betancourt of Venezuela. Browder said he stashed a portion of the stolen bonds outside of Miami and told FBI agents that he could recover a large amount of the bonds if they didn't arrest him. The agents declined his offer, noting in a report that Browder was a man with "a notorious reputation for past neutrality violations and other criminal activities," reported the special agent in charge in Miami.

Browder told agents that he received the bonds from unidentified Cubans who wanted him to export arms from Italy. During a search of his car, the agents found a letter from a man in Germany who said he had a buyer willing to buy the stolen bonds. The FBI also received a report that as much as $750,000 in bonds had surfaced in Havana, according to a report by Special Agent Jon Lenihan. Eventually, Browder was convicted of possessing the stolen bonds and sentenced to three years in prison. The FBI never learned what happened to all the bonds. In 1959, the *New York Times* reported that an insurance company bought back $1.4 million of the stolen bonds at ten cents on the dollar from unnamed underworld figures. Over the years, some of the securities turned up in China, Argentina and Australia.

The scheme took on aspects of a cloak-and-dagger operation. When Rabin was arrested by the FBI, he told Agents George Benjamin and James Ryan that he was to receive $2.5 million from a Castro representative, Alfredo Garcia, and then deliver the money to Castro's agents in Zurich, Rome and Venice who would identify themselves to Rabin by the number 26. Rabin said he passed one package of bonds to a Cuban agent in Rome.

Cotroni and Robert were named unindicted co-conspirators in Chicago because Canadian authorities arrested Cotroni after finding a large amount of heroin in an apartment that Cotroni had rented. Mannarino, Rothman, Rosden and Rabin were indicted by a federal grand jury in Chicago for bank and wire fraud in connection with the theft of $140,000 on the Canadian bonds. Mannarino was in Alberta, Canada, on a five-week hunting trip when the Royal Canadian Mounted Police arrested him as an undesirable alien because of his mob connections and deported him to the United States. He told the Mounties he was a "retired businessman" and left Canada on a plane for Las Vegas. The *Pittsburgh Post-Gazette* mocked Mannarino with a headline, "Canada Gives Heave-Ho to Sam Mannarino," in its October 14, 1966 edition. Mannarino was arrested by FBI agents at his office at the Ken Iron and Steel Company in New Kensington on July 3, 1959, and driven to the federal courthouse in Pittsburgh for arraignment in connection with the theft of bonds. He grew annoyed to see reporters and photographers waiting for him in the courthouse hallway. He was wearing dark sunglasses and partially covered his face with a handkerchief as he ducked into a closet and refused to come out after his arraignment to avoid having his photograph taken.

He pushed a photographer out of an elevator after he was released on $5,000 bond and threatened and cursed at reporters. The *Pittsburgh Post-Gazette* published a picture of the publicity-shy Mannarino lurking in the closet with the headline "Sam Mannarino Makes Bid as World's Greatest Actor."

12

CHICAGO

The weather in Chicago on Friday, January 5, 1962, was cold and forecast to get colder as the trial of Sam Mannarino, William Rabin, Norman Rothman and George Rosden began. It was below zero in the morning as fog hovered above the city. Light snow began falling onto the inch already on the ground as the winds coming off Lake Michigan covered the streets and vehicles with layers of ice.

The trial was expected to take a month, and some potential jurors were anxious to avoid being chosen to serve, leading U.S. District Court judge Joseph Sam Perry to accuse them of lying when they claimed that they would place more credence in the testimony of FBI agents over other witnesses. The judge admonished the prospective jurors by warning them, "I believe you are saying that you're favoring law enforcement just to evade jury duty," reported the *Chicago Sun Times*.

Perry was the son of an Alabama coal miner. He served in the U.S. Navy during World War I and was appointed to the federal court in 1951 by President Truman. In 1963, Perry experienced his fifteen minutes of fame when excavators unearthed an eleven-thousand-year-old mastodon skeleton in his backyard while workers were digging a pond.

The government's case was led by Assistant U.S. Attorney Donald Manion, a native of Chicago who served on a navy destroyer during the Korean War. The defense team included Vincent Casey, who represented Mannarino. Casey had a reputation in Pittsburgh as a mob lawyer who had defended members of Mannarino's organization on gambling charges and labor leader Nick Stirone, a mob associate, for accepting kickbacks from contractors on construction projects. He was a partner in a law firm headed by the late Charles Margiotti, a former Pennsylvania attorney general who had represented Pittsburgh Mafia boss John LaRocca and other racketeers and was a former business partner of Sam Mannarino.

Richard Gorman was an ex-cop and former assistant U.S. attorney who counted Chicago mobster Sam Giancana among his clients. Gordon had been indicted in 1960 for bribing a juror in a truck hijacking case involving several mobsters, but the trial ended in a hung jury. He was convicted in 1968 for income tax evasion, but the charge was dropped after it was revealed federal agents used an illegal wiretap to gain evidence to prosecute him. He was convicted of tax evasion in 1970 and sentenced to two years in prison.

Bradley Eben represented Rothman. Eban was a high-profile attorney who represented Chicago gangster Frank Nitti, who worked for Al Capone. It was Eben who delivered news to Nitti that he had been indicted by a grand jury for racketeering, conspiracy, mail fraud and extortion just before Nitti died by suicide in 1943.

Jury selection was completed on January 30, and testimony began with guards from Brinks Armored Trucks wheeling boxes stuffed with Canadian bonds into the courtroom. Manion began the government's case by explaining that the defendants were not charged with robbing the Canadian bank because that crime was outside U.S. jurisdiction—but were accused of trying to dispose of stolen property and committing fraud by using the bonds as collateral for loans.

One of the first witnesses to testify was Detective Sergeant Leslie Sterritt of the Brockville Police in Quebec, Canada, who explained that when he arrived at the bank the morning after the break-in, he found the vault room littered with shattered bricks, plaster and mortar—along with a fan that was still running—that the thieves used to clear the air, which reeked of smoke, charred wood and paper. The discovery of Rene Martin's identification quickly led investigators to the culprits.

Rabin and Rosden arrived in Switzerland on October 6, 1958, and met with officials of Leu and Company, a banking firm whose roots dated to 1755. They cashed in $15,000 worth of bonds and discussed future bond transfers. Rabin then met with officials at Credit Suisse bank in Basel, Switzerland, pledging $140,500 in bonds as collateral for a loan. In November, Credit Suisse learned the bonds were stolen, and Rabin made phone calls from Europe to Chicago, Montreal, Toronto, New York, Washington, D.C., and

Florida to tell his co-conspirators that the jig was up and authorities now knew about the plot, according to FBI records.

Rabin returned to the United States in January 1959 and redeemed $9,000 in bonds in New York City that he had already pledged to the Central National Bank in Chicago. When the bank learned the bonds had been cashed, officials notified the FBI, which triggered an investigation. Rabin, Rosden and Rothman were arrested in February and indicted in June. Sam Mannarino was arrested on July 2 in New Kensington and indicted by a federal grand jury in July.

After a series of bank officials testified, Manion called Kent Tomlinson, Rabin's friend and traveling companion in Europe, who was present at a meeting at a Florida motel in December 1958 in which Rabin, Mannarino and Pep Cotroni discussed ways how to convert the bonds into cash. Tomlinson worked as a dance instructor and Fuller Brush salesman before forming Kent Industries and inventing a "chicken plucking" machine that made removing feathers from chickens, turkeys and ducks easier than plucking them by hand. Tomlinson and Andrew Toti invented the machine in the 1940s, and Tomlin traveled the United States and the world selling the device. He married former beauty queen Dollye Culver at eighteen—she also was in Europe with Rabin and her husband but initially refused to talk to the FBI.

Kent Tomlinson also told the FBI the bizarre details of a cloak-and-dagger operation that entailed getting rid of the bonds. Rabin, Tomlinson said, met a mysterious individual in Chicago identified in FBI records as "Alfredo Garcia" who gave Rabin three packages of bonds that he was to give to Castro agents in Rome, Venice and Milan, Italy. The agents would identify themselves to Rabin by the number 26. Rabin arrived in Milan and passed the first package to a man in an airport bathroom, Tomlinson said.

The FBI considered Tomlinson "an important figure" in the investigation and wanted him to testify for the government. He told FBI agents Edward Kinzer Jr. and Robert Malone on February 14, 1959, that he was unaware of the bond deal and said the purpose of his trip to Europe with Rabin was to try to sell his invention to poultry processors.

In a second interview on May 3, 1959, Tomlinson retracted his prior statement and implicated Rothman, Mannarino, Controni and Rene Robert in the plot. He also gave the FBI phone bills showing calls that Rabin made to the other defendants. He made thirty calls to Montreal, sixteen to Washington, D.C., fourteen to New Kensington, seven to New York City and fifteen to Chicago.

Dollye Tomlinson also changed her mind about talking to agents and said she was with Rabin during most of their European trip and said Rabin never met anybody named Garcia as he claimed or any of Castro's agents in Rome or Milan.

Despite cooperating with the FBI and testifying before a federal grand jury, Tomlinson invoked the Fifth Amendment on the witness stand, fearing retribution from the mob after his wife received obscene phone calls before the trial began. He refused to acknowledge that he even knew Rabin, Rothman, Rosden or Mannarino or whether he had testified before a federal grand jury. Manion was stymied and frustrated. "I have no authority to compel him to answer, gentlemen, it's that simple," Judge Perry told the attorneys, according to a portion of the trial transcript contained in Rabin's appeal.

"Isn't it true, sir, that you advised me that you were fearful of your safety and that of your wife if you were to testify?" asked Manion. Tomlinson refused to respond, according to the transcript.

Mannarino was worried that Rabin would cut a plea deal with federal prosecutors and decided to kill him because "with Rabin out of the way" Mannarino likely wouldn't be convicted since Rabin would have been a key government witness. Mannarino assigned one of his henchmen, Abe Zeid, to kill Rabin, but Zeid dragged his feet and Mannarino rescinded the order, according to an office memorandum to Hoover from the Miami field office concerning the investigation. Rabin kept his mouth shut.

Mannarino was surprised to learn that Joe Merola, a man he thought enough of to consider bringing him into the Mafia, was a government witness. Merola testified that Mannarino lied to authorities when he claimed to be on hunting and fishing trip in Elk County, Pennsylvania, when he was in Florida. Sam and his brother Kelly had welcomed Merola into the fold, and Sam confided details of the bank heist to Merola without knowing he was working as a federal informant. As Merola took the witness stand, Mannarino stared at him and mouthed the word *weasel*.

Edward Lawton Smith, a Canadian underworld figure and sometime enforcer for the Mafia, was another informant. Smith served in the Canadian army during World War II. He killed a soldier in a fistfight and was court-martialed, convicted and sentenced to death by a firing squad. An appeals court overturned his conviction, and Smith returned to duty. After he was discharged, he became a courier for heroin dealers smuggling the drug into New York before becoming an informant. A biographical background report compiled by the CIA described Smith as "handsome," a "lady killer" and a sharp dresser who was married to a stripper.

Merola and Smith were key witnesses because they put Sam Mannarino in proximity to other conspirators in Canada, New York and Florida. Merola testified Mannarino and Cotroni were in Canada in August and September 1958 and in Florida in December with Cotroni, Rabin, Rene Robert and Norman Rothman. Smith testified he was present with Cotroni and Mannarino at a social gathering at the Café de Paris in New York City in June 1958 when Cotroni told him about the bonds. "I got a deal going down with some bonds supposed to go to Europe."

Five days after the New York gathering, Smith met Cotroni in a Montreal restaurant and said he had a buyer who offered to buy $3 million worth of bonds for eighteen cents on the dollar but Cotroni wanted twenty-one cents, according to trial transcripts.

"They [the buyers] want large denominations," Smith told Cotroni, according to the transcript. "They want as many bearer bonds as possible or the whole three million." Smith and Cotroni were in New York to conclude the sale when police grabbed them on their way to the meeting.

Smith was also known in the Canadian underworld as Joe Beard, Eddie O'Hare, Frank Ruso and Joe Franklin. He was from Nova Scotia and worked as an enforcer for the Canadian Mafia before becoming an informant for the U.S. Bureau of Narcotics and Dangerous Drugs. He implicated Cotroni in a deal to distribute 660 pounds of heroin valued at $8 million from Canada and into the United States. Federal agents estimated the amount of heroin Cotroni smuggled into the country was enough to create eight million individual doses for addicts.

The defense attorney tried to sidetrack Smith's testimony by making frequent objections and homing in on whether he was positive that the man he saw with Cotroni in New York was Mannarino. "I'm positive," Smith answered, according to the transcript.

When it came time for closing arguments, Manion told the jury that the defendants "are examples of daring and deceit with utter contempt for the laws under which we all live." Casey argued that the government's evidence was so weak that it couldn't sustain a conviction. "What was spun was a great international intrigue but it was a spider web, not strong enough to hold the government's evidence." Rabin's attorney Richard Gorman told jurors that when his client learned the bonds were stolen, he offered to make restitution to Leu and Company. "Knowledge of the alleged crime is an essential element, and that hasn't been proven."

Mannarino and Rosden were found not guilty. Rothman was cleared by the judge on a direct verdict of acquittal. Rabin was convicted and sentenced to ten years in prison. Cotroni and Robert had been charged in Canada with possession of heroin in addition to the theft of the bonds. Cotroni was sentenced to a total of seventeen years in prison on the drug charges and for possessing stolen bonds. Robert was sentenced to eight years. Stepanoff was never charged in the Brockville heist, and Winford was killed in what police suspected was a mob hit.

After the verdict was announced, an elated Mannarino rushed to a payphone in the federal courthouse to tell his wife in New Kensington the good news. "Why are you crying?" he asked her. "I'm coming home." He later admitted to an FBI agent that he would have pleaded guilty to the charges if the government had offered a two-year prison term, reported the *Pittsburgh Press*.

"He asserted that it was most certainly true that he was willing to take a two-year rap instead of facing nine weeks of aggravation in connection with a trial," wrote Special Agent Thomas Forsyth III. "He said he would do 'two years vacation and be glad to get the rest.'"

13

CHICKEN FEED

Sam Mannarino wasn't a defendant, but his presence loomed over the pending trial against his son-in-law, Victor Carlucci, Norman Rothman, Stuart Sutor, Joseph Giordano and Daniel "Speedo" Hanna. They were all charged with attempting to smuggle stolen military weapons to Fidel Castro in Cuba. Jurors at the federal courthouse in Pittsburgh were surprised as prosecutors began hauling an arsenal of weapons into the courtroom and stacking them against the walls. There were ninety-two M-1 rifles, twenty-four carbines, four machine guns, a .22-caliber rifle and two dismantled .50-caliber machine guns that were not among the confiscated weapons. "Although the federal government was not able to prove it, there is no question that Samuel Mannarino was part of the conspiracy," read a 1961 FBI report. Instead of Sam Mannarino, federal prosecutors Hubert Teitelbaum and Daniel Snyder portrayed Carlucci as the leader of the conspiracy. Federal prosecutors subpoenaed Mannarino and his wife, Rose, to appear before a grand jury investigating the case but Mannarino refused to sign a waiver of immunity that would have allowed the government to use his grand jury testimony against Carlucci at trial. Rose Mannarino pleaded illness and admitted herself to a hospital. The government wanted to question the Mannarinos about Carlucci's whereabouts on November 4, 1958, the day the guns were flown from Remich Airport. "It is for reasons we believe in the government's best interests that we have excused Mannarino from testifying at this time," said Teitelbaum, according to the *Pittsburgh Press*.

The federal government called seventy-three individuals, including witnesses who saw them unloading a truck and then loading the airplane with bundles wrapped in burlap. The guns weren't the most compelling evidence prosecutors presented. It was the "chicken feed"—kernels of corn, wheat and oats that were found in the burlap bags in the plane's fuselage—that matched products from a feed store where the bags were purchased. The dirt found in the plane matched the dirt along the runway at the airport, according to FBI analysts who testified.

Members of the Mannarino organization waiting outside federal court in Pittsburgh. From left to right are Kelly Mannarino, Victor Carlucci, Joe Giordano and Daniel "Speedo" Hanna. *From the* Valley News Dispatch.

Prosecutors tied the defendants to the scheme through phones calls they made back and forth to each other during the planning stages. FBI agents testified about calls made to Cuba, Miami, New York and New Kensington to link the defendants to the plot. Hotel and motel records tracked the whereabouts of the suspects in Florida and the Pittsburgh area, according to the *Pittsburgh Sun-Telegraph*.

The prosecutors noted that Joseph Merola was in regular contact with Carlucci, Rothman and Pessolano, and they also presented as evidence toll records of calls between Sutor and Carlucci the night before the plane took off and between Sutor and Pessolano and Carlucci and Norman Rothman. Pessolano was named as an unindicted co-conspirator, which meant the grand jury found that he was part of the criminal conspiracy but his behavior fell short of an actual crime.

Prosecutors recounted for the jury how the scheme began with a telephone call from Rothman to Pessolano asking him to lease an aircraft and hire a pilot for the gunrunning mission. Pessolano admitted at trial that he had lied to the FBI about the source of the call.

"The call that came from Rothman I believe was local in nature and not long distance and it was probably made from his home in Surfside, Florida," Pessolano testified. "There was no mention of money during the first call but there was a request for a pilot."

Pessolano was a key witness, but his credibility suffered after he admitted lying to the FBI and before a federal grand jury to protect himself from implicating Mannarino.

"Pessolano is the only person…in a position to implicate Top-Hoodlum Sam Mannarino in the gun running conspiracy," wrote FBI director J. Edgar Hoover to the special agent in charge of the Miami field office. He added that the Miami physician was "believed to be the only witness who can supply sufficient evidence to insure the conviction of Mannarino son-in-law, Victor E. Carlucci, also under indictment."

Pessolano had treated Mannarino when Mannarino visited Miami and later provided him with cocaine to ease the pain he was experiencing from colon cancer, according to a report filed by Special Agent Richard Gordon Douce on February 19, 1959, and to an office memorandum sent to Hoover from the special agent in charge of the Pittsburgh office dated July 28, 1959.

The jury also heard testimony from Fausto Gomez, a former Cuban Air Force pilot who was held at gunpoint by Merola to force him to fly the plane to Cuba, and from pilot Charles "Pete" Smith, the first man Pessolano offered the job.

While Pessolano was under pressure from the FBI to tell the truth, others were pressuring him to keep quiet. He received a phone call from a Miami attorney who represented underworld figures advising him to invoke the Fifth Amendment against self-incrimination when he testified before a federal grand jury or at trial. Pessolano replied he would "make up his own mind" what to do when the time came, reported Special Agent Richard Gordon Douce. Pessolano was worried that Sam Mannarino would kill him after the FBI notified police in Miami about a potential threat. Pessolano died in 1983.

Only one of the five defendants testified. Giordano told the jury he bought the burlap bags to cover newly planted grass seed in his yard. His yard was ten feet wide and twenty feet long—too small to need that many bags, argued prosecutors. An FBI search of his property uncovered ninety-nine bags hidden in the cellar of his home. Another forty were spread across his lawn. Another six were stashed under a porch, and three were in the trunk of his car.

The prosecution disputed Giordano's testimony by calling in a horticulturist, who testified that the rye grass Giordano had seeded his yard with would have germinated within seven to ten days after planting, and by November 4, 1958, he no longer would have a need to cover the yard with burlap.

The defense complained about the prejudicial news coverage of the trial and stories linking the defendants to the Mannarino mob in New Kensington. They asked visiting judge Roger T. Foley of Las Vegas, Nevada, to declare a mistrial after nine jurors admitted they had glanced at headlines about the trial in newspapers but said they never read the articles. Foley's words to the jury here are taken from a partial transcript of the trial contained in an appeal:

> *Now I am going to ask this question of all of you: From your glances or perusal of any of the headlines or of any other matter contained in any newspaper or anything you might have heard on a television broadcast or radio broadcast, is there anyone here who has any doubt in his mind or her mind but that he or she could try this case and base his or her verdict entirely upon the evidence brought into court and admitted here and uninfluenced by any outside communication of any kind whatsoever? Now don't be afraid to say so....If you have any qualms about it, if there is anything you have heard outside the courtroom concerning any person connected with this trial which you have reason to believe would make it difficult for you to give any of the defendants in this case a fair trial, please don't hesitate to say so.*

None of the jurors spoke up, so the judge continued the trial.

Defense lawyers Vito Rich, Vincent Casey and Michael von Moschzisker told the jury during the closing arguments that there was no evidence the defendants knew the cargo was stolen guns or destined for Cuba. "The mere fact that these men loaded the plane does not show they had knowledge of the destination of the aircraft or they were stolen," said attorney Vincent Casey. He said the prosecution's case was based on "the flimsiest type of evidence, conjecture and guesses," said the *Pittsburgh Sun Telegraph*. Hanna was "nothing more than an innocent chauffeur" who just drove the van to the airport and was unaware there were guns inside. Giordano's supplied shipment of guns was legitimate, and prosecutors never presented any evidence Rothman conspired with anybody.

The defense attorneys argued the government never presented any evidence that the cargo was guns, because they were covered in burlap.

As far as the phone calls, Casey said Carlucci lived with his in-laws, Sam and Rose Mannarino, and the calls could have been made by his father-in-law. In addition, no evidence was presented as to the subject of the phone calls. Merola, the defense argued, "was just there. Sutor didn't know the guns were stolen."

U.S. Attorney Hubert Teitelbaum said the pretext that the plane was to be used for a hunting and fishing trip was unbelievable. "Is this the way an innocent hunting trip starts?" He said that's why Pessolano asked Rothman point-blank if the cargo was guns, the *Pittsburgh Sun-Telegraph* reported.

The men were convicted and sentenced to five years in prison. Defense attorneys for the five men appealed the convictions to the Third Circuit Court of Appeals, which upheld the verdicts. After he went to prison, Sutor personally filed a motion for a new trial, arguing that his attorney refused to allow him to testify since the attorneys were hired by Carlucci likely through his father-in-law. The judges denied Sutor's motion and pointed out that he was given a chance to speak at his sentencing but remained mute.

The FBI learned that Hanna was unhappy with the way the Mannarino organization reneged on its promise about caring for his family if he was convicted. During his arraignment after his arrest, Hanna approached FBI special agent Thomas Forsyth III and spoke "earnestly, courteously and at length," according to a memo sent to J. Edgar Hoover from the special agent in charge in Pittsburgh. Hanna told Forsyth he was upset that promised financial support was not forthcoming and was unhappy about being separated from his ten-year-old son.

Forsyth traveled to the federal penitentiary in Lewisburg, Pennsylvania to recruit Hanna as an informant ,but Hanna had a change of heart. He was in hock to the Mannarinos for several thousand dollars in gambling debts and hoped they would cancel the obligation if he remained silent.

While four of the defendants were serving time, Joseph Merola was sprung from a prison in Florida, which would remain a secret for fourteen years.

14

MYSTERY MAN

Joseph Raymond Merola walked out of a federal prison in Florida in 1963 a free man after serving fourteen months of his five-year prison sentence. President John F. Kennedy pardoned the former used car salesman–turned jewel thief in a decision that would remain a secret until 1975, when it was revealed Merola was working as an FBI informant at the same time he was on trial for gunrunning. The U.S. Department of Justice forwarded a petition for executive clemency to White House pardons attorney Reed Cozart on April 26, 1962, with a recommendation that it be approved.

Merola was accused of selling out his co-defendants after Norman Rothman had his prison sentence vacated in 1975 after alleging that the government knew that Merola was a government informant during the trial and accused him of revealing defense strategies to federal prosecutors, which helped them obtain convictions. Richard Thornburgh, then U.S. attorney for the Western District of Pennsylvania, never challenged Rothman's petition, but two years later, the government opposed similar motions filed by Victor Carlucci and Daniel "Speedo" Hanna, who had already served their sentences.

The case was prosecuted by then U.S. attorney Hubert Teitelbaum, a former FBI agent, and his assistant Daniel Snyder, who were later appointed federal judges by President Richard Nixon in 1970. Both men swore in affidavits that they were unaware that Merola was a government informant and said he never provided any information that compromised the fairness of the trial, reported the *Pittsburgh Post-Gazette*.

Attorneys Vincent Casey and Irving Green, who represented Carlucci and Hanna, also accused the CIA of interceding on Merola's behalf because Merola served as a CIA informant as well, providing information to the agency concerning Fidel Castro. "The government has protected him," Green told the *Pittsburgh Post-Gazette*.

Declassified FBI and CIA records released under the Presidential Assassinations Act revealed Merola's dual roles as an informant for both agencies. Even though Merola had been a CIA source since the early 1960s, according to declassified CIA records, the spy agency was still suspicious of him but wanted to use his contacts in Cuba, the Mafia, the Dominican Republic and Nicaragua. CIA reports characterized him as a "notorious smuggler, gun runner and general no goodnik," according to a CIA memo from its Domestic Collection Division.

In a 1977 letter from the CIA to the House Select Committee on Assassinations, the agency tried to keep its relationship with Merola at arm's length, saying, "Merola was a voluntary source of foreign intelligence. We are obliged to listen politely, take down his information for transmittal to the appropriate area desk and make absolutely no promise for future contact."

A previous CIA document described Merola's relationship differently. In January 1974, the chief of the Domestic Collection Division wrote that Merola "has passed to this office some very reliable information." Merola was not a CIA agent "but has been a DCD contact since the early sixties."

Merola provided the CIA with information about the internal politics within the Castro government and about the personal rivalries between Castro's military leaders. He warned the agency in 1959 of Cuban plans to send insurgents into Panama and the Dominican Republic to foment revolution. A Cuban force attempted to stage a coup in Panama on April 24, 1959, but was repulsed by the Panamanian National Guard. Then in June, another Cuban-backed contingent of fifty-six men landed in the Dominican Republic, but all were killed by army troops.

Merola told CIA agents that he had met brothers Fidel and Raul Castro in May 1959 and informed the CIA that Cuba was planning to invade Panama, according to a CIA report titled *Caribbean Political and Revolutionary Activities* dated December 24, 1959. When Merola arrived in Miami from one of his visits to Cuba, he was questioned by customs inspectors and told them he was trying to sell heavy equipment to the Cuban government and boasted of his friendship with Castro, even displaying a photograph of Castro and Merola together, according to a memo sent to Hoover from Pittsburgh.

Merola was born in Turtle Creek, a blue-collar town along the Monongahela River, and grew up in Wilkinsburg, a small city adjacent to Pittsburgh. He served in the U.S. Marine Corps from 1942 until 1945 in an aircraft squadron. After the war, he owned a used car lot that served as a cover for his criminal activities. He was arrested for robbing South Carolina used car dealers, claiming they could buy vehicles in Pittsburgh at cheap prices and then steering them to a specific hotel, where he relieved them of their cash.

He graduated to being a jewel thief, making the FBI list of top jewel thieves in the nation. He was a suspect in high-end heists, including the $660,000 theft of jewels from a safe at the William Penn Hotel in Pittsburgh in 1954 as well as burglaries in New York City, Chicago, Miami Beach and Hot Springs, Arkansas, according to FBI documents.

A salesman for Oscar Heyman and Brothers in New York City arrived at the William Penn and placed a case filled with gems and jewelry in the hotel's "foolproof" vault. When the salesman went to retrieve the merchandise the next day, his case was missing. The master key to the vault was left in an unlocked drawer, making it easy for anyone who knew where the key was located to remove the key and open the vault door.

Detectives theorized that the thief rented hotel safe deposit boxes over time to familiarize himself with the layout and made a duplicate key of each box he rented. He then removed the master key from the desk drawer to enter the vault and began pilfering the boxes until he located the one with the gems. The theft was one of twenty-two jewel robberies in southwestern Pennsylvania that year in which $2 million was stolen, reported the *Pittsburgh Press*.

A former colleague in crime of Merola's described him to the FBI as a gutless braggart who didn't have the courage to participate in an actual heist and mainly planned the robberies and fenced the jewelry. For example, he told agents how he and Merola planned to rob a Yellow Cab payroll in Washington, D.C., but after Merola cased the job and provided the guns and masks, he didn't have the courage to follow through so the heist was called off. The coconspirator also recounted a planned jewelry robbery that Merola set up in Kansas City, but Merola got "cold feet" at the last minute and abandoned the plan, according to a report filed by FBI special agent John Portella of Pittsburgh.

Merola was also suspected in the theft of $70,000 worth of jewels from a salesman in New York City, according to FBI reports. He was a suspect in the theft of $75,000 in diamonds in Pittsburgh as well as $126,000 in gems in Chicago and another haul of $117,000 in Florida. He was suspected of stealing a total of $1 million in negotiable securities in robberies in Chicago, New York City and Hot Springs, Arkansas. Merola made trips to Cuba to sell jewelry and was involved in the theft of more than $179,000 worth of furs in Reno, Nevada, according to a memo sent to Hoover from the Pittsburgh field office in 1961.

Merola became informant MM-T-1 after he told an assistant U.S. attorney in Miami that he could provide information about the Mannarino brothers and the theft of the weapons from the National Guard Armory in Canton, Ohio, in 1958. The FBI was desperate to obtain evidence against Sam Mannarino so they could charge him in the plot since others involved in the plot were afraid to testify against him. "You're on the right track. All you have to do is put me off the record and I'll tell you the whole story," Merola told Special Agent George E. Davis Jr., who attended the March 30, 1959 meeting.

Merola spoke Spanish and was a pilot, which helped him operate in South Florida, Cuba and Central America. He had been warmly received by Castro after the revolution for his help in arming Castro's forces. He was also someone you dared not trust. Even though he helped Castro, he flew Fulgencio Batista and his brother-in-law into exile when Castro entered Havana, according to the book *Jukebox Empire*.

Merola approached the CIA in August 1961 with information about Cuban revolutionary Che Guevara that he had received from a contact who was a Brazilian politician and friend of Guevara, according to an account of a February 8, 1961 meeting with Justin Gleichauf of the CIA's Contact Division Support. Guevara was born in Argentina and joined Castro's revolutionary movement before going to Bolivia to foment revolution there. He became an important leader in the movement and served for a time in the Castro government before going to Bolivia, where a United States–trained Bolivian army unit captured him on October 8, 1967, and executed Guevara the next day.

Merola relished his role as a CIA informant but exaggerated his position by claiming he was an agent, much to the chagrin of the agency. He was overheard on an FBI wiretap at Ciro's, a North Miami Beach restaurant, telling mob associates that he worked for the intelligence agency "on the Cuban situation" and had amassed an arsenal of weapons that included machine guns, hand grenades and silencers. An official of the agency's Domestic Collection Division complained in a memo dated March 11, 1974, that Merola "had taken advantage of his agency contacts in an inappropriate manner to the potential embarrassment of the CIA. We would, accordingly, appreciate that this be given consideration in your assessment of the advantage of your contact with him." The agency temporarily halted contact with Merola. "We are aware of his unsavory record but he has from time to time produced information of interest," according to the CIA memo.

Merola had a penchant for convincing people he was a CIA agent. Frank Sturgis, an ex-Marine, former soldier and mercenary who fought with Castro, told government investigators that Merola was working undercover for the agency. Sturgis was born Frank Fiorini and fought alongside Castro during the revolution and afterward was appointed director of intelligence for the fledgling Cuban Air Force before Sturgis broke with Castro over communism. Sturgis was better known for his role in breaking into the Democratic Party campaign offices in the Watergate apartment complex, which led to the resignation of President Nixon.

"Joe was an undercover agent," Sturgis said. "He was closely associated with the government. He did have an association with the CIA. I know Joe was very involved in the revolution," according to a statement Sturgis gave to the House Select Committee on Assassinations. Merola appeared as a witness against Sam Mannarino at a trial in Chicago and began providing the FBI with information about their criminal operations and personal lives. Sam Mannarino predicted in February 1962 that Merola would be dead within a month after his release from prison. Then a month later, he speculated that "a prisoner in a southern penitentiary" would receive a presidential pardon and that he was "going to get him," according to a report filed with the FBI Pittsburgh field office in April. Herbert J. Miller, an assistant attorney general in the Criminal Division, wrote to J. Edgar Hoover on April 26, 1962, inquiring whether Sam Mannarino should be charged with threatening a government witness.

The FBI received a tip from the Bureau of Narcotics and Dangerous Drugs, now known as the Drug Enforcement Administration, that the alleged killers were from New Kensington and were staying at the Eden Roc Hotel in Miami. The men were not identified, but one individual fit the description of Abe Zeid, a reputed enforcer for the Mannarinos. Merola sluffed off the threat, telling FBI agents if he was killed, they would be knocking the next day on Sam Mannarino's door.

Merola was forever the con man. He approached William Pawley, former U.S. ambassador to Brazil, in 1960 about ways to destabilize the Cuban economy. Before World War II, Pawley helped organize the Flying Tigers, a group of civilian American volunteer pilots flying for China following the

Japanese invasion. Pawley had an interest in Cuba and was an avowed anti-communist, so he listened to what Merola had to say. Pawley tried to record the meeting, but his tape recorder malfunctioned.

Merola met with Pawley on April 9, 1960, and proposed flooding Cuba with $50 million in counterfeit pesos to destabilize the nation's currency, but Pawley would have to supply $50,000 to finance the scheme.

Merola had a social relationship with an assistant U.S. attorney in Miami who refused to file charges against Merola for planning a $100,000 jewelry store robbery even after Merola admitted he planned it. The State of Illinois paid Merola over $50,000 as an informant even though some officials questioned what he did to earn the money. Merola was known as a "Super Stool," and state officials were vague about the work Merola performed while working for the Illinois Bureau of Investigation. Using the alias Joe Sanello, Merola worked undercover investigating organized crime, while he was working for the state, he was arrested for two jewel heists, according to an account in the *Chicago Sun Times* in 1976.

He was charged in 1973 with stealing $20,000 in jewels in Great Neck, New York, during a home invasion, but intercession by the Drug Enforcement Administration resulted in Merola being sentenced to three years' probation. That same year, he was arrested for stealing $20,000 in jewels, but federal agents again helped Merola escape prosecution.

"There are some types of informants you can't control," said an Illinois law enforcement official. "They do good work for various reasons. Money, excitement, or so on. He won't come up with anything until he gets paid or until he gets caught," the official told the *Sun-Times*.

After he was pardoned, Merola called the *Pittsburgh Press* to complain about a reference in a story about his pardon describing him as a "convict." Merola said he prepared the papers for his commutation on his own writing "that justice would not be served with my being in prison." He claimed he was involved in the Bay of Pigs debacle and hinted he still worked for the CIA.

"Just say that I'm extremely interested in promoting democracy and that I'm an All-American boy. Sure, I tried to help Castro," Merola said. "But don't forget. The government was on his side also. Nobody knew he would turn out to be a communist," he told the *Pittsburgh Press* in 1963.

15

OPERATION CRUSADE

Residents throughout racket-ridden Westmoreland County were fed up with the Mafia, the Mannarinos and the city's reputation as a mecca for organized crime, so the clergy decided to turn to God for help. The Mannarino organization was under siege by the U.S. Department of Justice, the FBI, the IRS and the press in the 1950s and 1960s. Then the clergy piled on. Like zealous Old Testament prophets, ministers banded together to form Operation Crusade to break the Mafia's grip on vice.

The pulpit became the new weapon in the war against organized crime. Ministers from various Protestant denominations went after the political ring that controlled the Westmoreland County Courthouse in Greensburg, the city of Monessen in the southern end of the county and in the small towns in between. But the pastors viewed New Kensington as a modern-day Sodom and Gomorrah rolled into one. Genesis tells the tale of how God destroyed the cities by fire and brimstone for their wicked ways. Since fire and brimstone were not an option, the ministers began their own political movement, targeting specific officials and embarrassing some of them who were members of their churches.

The crusade's formal name was the United Commission on Social Action, and it waged political guerrilla war against Westmoreland County district attorney Alexander Sculco, who lived in New Kensington; his chief of detectives, Arthur "Buddy" Turner; local judges Edward Bauer, John O'Connell and Richard Laird; along with state senator John Dent. The ministers accused these officials of being in cahoots with the Mannarinos,

John Dent. The Mannarinos bankrolled his election campaigns for the Pennsylvania Senate. He was later elected to Congress. *U.S. House of Representatives.*

but the clergymen often found themselves at odds with their congregants who were social and political acquaintances of these officials.

Turner became a frequent target. His ancestors arrived on the *Mayflower*, and he had a great-great-grandfather who was killed during the Civil War, according to a 2021 story in the *Mon Valley Messenger*. Turner drew particular attention from the ministers. On a salary of $3,600 a year, Turner bought a twenty-five-room house in 1948, according to the *Monessen Daily Independent*. The house was constructed entirely of stone and resembled an English manor. He also purchased a new car every year and spent two months in Florida every winter. One FBI informant said that Turner had amassed so much money that he "needed a bailing machine" to handle the cash. Turner had a record of sex offenses and never arrested a racketeer during his eighteen-year tenure and conducted few gambling raids. It's not known how Turner became a detective and attained so much power, but his reign as the political boss of Westmoreland County ended with his death in 1959.

Sculco may have been the district attorney, but Turner was the power behind the throne. Turner told a writer for *Collier's* magazine that his nickname was "Buddy" because "I'm everybody's buddy." Turner decided who could run for judge and ruled that any candidate must first have served as district attorney. At that point, every current and former judge had served in that office.

"The importance of the District Attorney's office cannot be overemphasized since every judge in Westmoreland County was formerly a District Attorney or an assistant in that office and have been part of the same organization," wrote Special Agent Francis Allison in a 1962 report on crime conditions in western Pennsylvania.

Pressure from the ministers was so strong that Kelly Mannarino was forced to curtail gambling. Slot machines disappeared. Punch boards vanished from bars. No more backroom high-stakes poker games. Bookie parlors and horse rooms closed. In 1951, the Pennsylvania State Police swept through New Kensington's red-light district rounding up pimps and prostitutes since local cops and county detectives could not be trusted to enforce the law.

Operation Crusade's leader was the Reverend Allen Howes, who accused Sculco of brazenly condoning "prostitution, pandering and gambling" and "who retains in office a chief of detectives with an evil sex record and who consorts openly with criminals of national reputation," a reference to the Mannarino brothers. "There is no excuse for men who are elected to enforce the law and then refuse that responsibility—either because of indifference, ineptitude or collusion," Howes told the *Pittsburgh Press.* "They should be removed from office by legal means and replaced by men of honor."

Another of the crusade's leaders was a short, feisty journalist named Ruth Love, whose son became an FBI agent. Love investigated mobsters and elected officials and turned the information over to the ministers, who used her findings as grist for their Sunday sermons. She provided federal prosecutors with information about vote fraud in Westmoreland County and testified before a federal grand jury that led to indictments. "We are not reformers," said Love. "We aren't telling you can't drink or play slot machines but we are saying you shouldn't have to pay tribute to corrupt public officials to do so," reported the *Monessen Daily Independent.*

Howes cited Sculco's "tragic record" as a prosecutor. "Westmoreland County has, as it had for nearly 20 years, a district attorney who brazenly condones prostitution, pandering and gambling," Howes charged. "In Westmoreland County dead men and women leave their graves on election day and vote, once twice, thrice," the *Pittsburgh Post-Gazette* reported.

Sculco retaliated against the ministers by having the state police investigate Operation Crusade, charging it was backed by the Communist Party. Senator Dent claimed Operation Crusade was a political organization and had raised $60,000 in an unsuccessful attempt to defeat him for reelection to the Pennsylvania Senate and therefore should be required to disclose the names of its contributors. "Although they are men and women who plead poverty, they seem to have sufficient funds to print the most scurrilous, slanderous and libelous literature ever in political campaigns in Westmoreland County's history," Dent complained to the *Pittsburgh Post-Gazette.*

Sculco was unnerved by the ministers' attacks, especially after the crusade claimed credit for defeating Dent's bid to become a Westmoreland County commissioner. He demanded Howes resign as the leader of Operation Crusade. "If Reverend Howes wants to go into politics and gain control of the Republican Party of Westmoreland County he should resign from the ministry and get into politics and not hide behind the cloak of decency," said Dent in a story reported by the *Daily Mail* in Monongahela. Howes was pleased by Dent's defeat, saying, "I am gratified to realize that Operation Crusade had some degree of success in defeating Dent," reported the *Monessen Daily Independent.*

Sculco met with Howes and a delegation of ministers to discuss the investigation, but nothing was accomplished at the meeting because Sculco complained that the ministers didn't present any evidence that would allow him to take action. "Ministers should attend to their spiritual duties instead of politics," complained Sculco to the *Connellsville Daily Courier.*

The ministers were in an uproar over Sculco's request for an investigation by the state police. Governor John Fine agreed to meet with Howes, but when Howes asked Fine if he had issued an order to the state police to investigate Operation Crusade, Fine became angry and refused to answer. "I do not propose to sit here and be cross examined by you," reported the *Pittsburgh Post-Gazette*, which later castigated Sculco in an editorial, writing, "a clue to the motivation behind the inquiry is provided by the State Police admission that the questions they have been asking were drawn up by Westmoreland County District Attorney Alexander Sculco."

Fine's motivation was suspect since he pardoned Pittsburgh boss John LaRocca two days before Christmas in 1954 so LaRocca could escape deportation to Sicily after the government ruled that he was an undesirable alien because of two criminal convictions as a young man. The pardon was approved on November 27, 1954, but was dated May 1954. Fine delayed announcing the pardon for seven months until deportation hearings were underway.

The pardon cleansed his criminal convictions, giving the government no legal grounds to deport him. The Pennsylvania Board of Pardons recommended LaRocca's exoneration, writing that "he has conducted himself as an honorable and upright citizen in legitimate business since his conviction in 1939," although LaRocca was knee-deep in organized crime. The FBI, in one of its reports, said bookmakers in Pittsburgh suspected the pardon cost LaRocca between $50,000 and $100,000 before Fine left office on December 31, 1954.

The ministerial efforts to rid the county of vice came at a price. Reverend Howes had a nervous breakdown. The Reverend Doctor Wilford Noble, a Baptist minister from New Kensington, received anonymous telephone calls threatening him with death. "You got to keep your mouth shut, brother, or you will get bumped off," reported the *Pittsburgh Sun-Telegraph.*

"I do believe they are trying to strike fear into the hearts of anti-racket elements," Noble said.

When New Kensington police chief John Bettor had the temerity to ignore the mayor's order against staging gambling raids and closed a Mannarino-run joint, he was fired by Mayor Ray Gardlock. Noble led public efforts to reinstate him. More than one thousand residents turned out for a public meeting, which resulted in Bettor's reinstatement, although he eventually was replaced as chief by a Mannarino henchman and demoted to patrolman, reported the *Pittsburgh Sun-Telegraph*.

Captain Carl Anderson of the Salvation Army in New Kensington said it was the Christian duty of ministers to "stamp them out. We cannot let honest people suffer because of corrupt politicians or vicious underworld characters," reported the *Pittsburgh Post-Gazette*.

The Reverend William P. Cooke, a Presbyterian pastor in Greensburg who also was active in the movement, was barred from entering his church and his salary was withheld until he resigned as pastor because of his involvement in Operation Crusade, reported the *Pittsburgh Post-Gazette*. Judge Edward Bauer left the Methodist Church in Jeannette and joined the First Presbyterian Church in Greensburg because of the involvement in Operation Crusade by his pastor, the Reverend Samuel Ford. "Judge Bauer did not assign a reason for leaving our church but there is not the slightest doubt that he was displeased because of our activity in Operation Crusade," Ford told the *Pittsburgh Post-Gazette*.

The Reverend J. Nelson Jackaway, another Presbyterian pastor, was fired from the Rehoboth Presbyterian Church in Belle Veron in Westmoreland County's Monongahela Valley because of his involvement in the organization. Jackaway took to the pulpit to denounce local politicians who protected the racketeers. His stand upset some members of his congregation, who asked the Redstone Presbytery to investigate Jackaway after he refused a request by members of his congregation to tone down his rhetoric. They complained Jackaway showed a lack of tact and discretion in dealing with certain politicians, according to the *Valley Independent* in Monessen.

Jackaway said it was his duty as a minister to stem the spread of vice in the county and said members of the political ring that controlled the Westmoreland County Courthouse persuaded members of his church to silence him, according to the *Monessen Daily Independent*.

The controversy attracted so much unwanted publicity that members of the church asked the Monessen newspaper to stop reporting on the issue because it was a "very personal situation and really a family matter. The commission is doing its very best to resolve the difficulties and we would appreciate very much if you would refrain from giving the story any more space in your newspaper," according to a letter sent to the newspaper, The newspaper refused the request arguing the public had a right to know if outside forces were behind the move to oust Jackaway.

The Presbytery completed its investigation and absolved Jackaway, ruling that Operation Crusade was not the source of the church's internal problems. Nevertheless, Jackaway was ordered that "discussion of the activities of Operation Crusade...be kept from the pulpit and all church activities," reported the Monessen newspaper.

In response to pressure from Operation Crusade, Sculco ordered gambling raids throughout the county, but they were nothing more than a public-relations stunt. Police hit out-of-the way joints, resulting in no major arrests, and his raiders never touched any places in New Kensington.

While Presbyterian, Methodist, Episcopal, Baptist and Church of God clergy dominated the ranks of Operation Crusade, conspicuously missing from the movement were Catholic priests. Father Owen Kirby, pastor of St. Leonard's Catholic Church in Monessen, decried Operation Crusade, comparing it to Stalin's purges.

"Moderate gambling is not a sin any more than moderate drinking," Kirby said. "But gambling, which is no sin only in some states, like Pennsylvania, where the unsepulchered [sic] ghosts of Jonathan Edward and other of the blue-nosed Puritans of New England still rule. Anything that is not forbidden by the Ten Commandments ought not to be made illegal without grave reason," reported the Pittsburgh Press.

Honest officials who bucked the Mafia did so at their own risk. Westmoreland County's Elections Director Catherine Mitchell gave the FBI copies of the voting records of Mafia boss Domenick Anzalone and ended up under arrest accused of tampering with official records. Anzalone voted in elections even though he was not a U.S. citizen, but when Sculco and Turner learned what Mitchell had done, they were livid.

"After I cooperated with the FBI to enable them to take photostats of Dominick Anzalone's registration records my troubles in the courthouse began," she said. "You'll pay for this," warned Judge Edward Bauer. "When we're through with you, you'll have a criminal record," reported the Pittsburgh Post-Gazette. "I'll make her sorry for this," added Judge John O'Connell.

Judges Bauer and Laird issued an order impounding the voting records and seized the key to her office. When agents returned to the courthouse to get the original records to present as evidence at Anzalone's trial, the documents were missing. Turner had ordered a janitor to burn them. Mitchell had previously complained to Sculco and Bauer of voting irregularities, but they refused to conduct an investigation.

When it came time to seek Mitchell's indictment from the grand jury, Sculco empaneled three grand juries to indict Mitchell, but each time the panel refused to charge her because jurors ruled there was no evidence that she broke any laws. To put the controversy to rest, Sculco and Bauer offered Mitchell a deal. If she confessed and resigned, they wouldn't seek a jail sentence. She refused, so they agreed to let her resign and dropped the charges. The *Valley Independent* in Monessen mentioned in an editorial the "somewhat unique" system of justice in Westmoreland County. "If the charges against Mrs. Mitchell are shushed up and the D.A. refuses to bring her to trial, the public can hardly be blamed for suspecting the worst."

New Kensington's local newspaper, the *Daily Dispatch*, published editorials castigating city and county officials for their dereliction of duty, writing that the mayor and police department of New Kensington were "owned lock, stock and barrel" by the Mannarinos and an embarrassment to the public. The paper's editorial writers charged Westmoreland County was "in the clutches of the county politico-racket machine." When District Attorney Richard McCormick ran for reelection in 1961, the *Dispatch* accused him of having the nerve to ask voters for another term, calling him a "creature of a corrupt" political system and "unfit to hold office."

The city council tried to curtail the negative news coverage of New Kensington when the *Dispatch* and the *Valley Daily News* in neighboring Tarentum in Allegheny County tried to expand their circulation in New Kensington. The council passed an anti-littering law that included a provision to prevent newspaper canvassers from going door-to-door circulating flyers seeking new customers. Gardlock was described in news articles as a "tool" of the brothers and was fed up with the editorial heat. An appeals court judge struck down the law. The *Daily Dispatch* was founded in 1919 and in 1960 was purchased by the *Valley Daily News* in Tarentum.

16

ALCOA AND THE MOB

*A*n economic pall settled over New Kensington in the late 1960s when Alcoa executives became displeased with its employees' productivity and issued an ultimatum to its workforce. If employees wanted Alcoa to remain in the city, union workers must agree to an end to incentive pay, accept layoffs and increase aluminum production; otherwise, the plant would close.

In 1966, the union agreed to the demands in exchange for Alcoa spending $4.5 million for plant modernization in what was billed as a "Save the Plant" movement. The *Pittsburgh Post-Gazette* heralded the deal in a banner headline on March 22, 1966, that read, "Pact Keeps Alcoa Plant Open." But the agreement would be short-lived.

In addition to eliminating incentive pay, the union saw its ranks reduced from 2,200 to 1,700. Aluminum production declined over the next several years, and by 1970, writing was on the wall. There would be no future for Alcoa in New Kensington. On March 31, 1971, the plant closed. Alcoa's earnings declined that year during the first quarter from more than $39 million to nearly $18 million. John D. Harper, CEO of Alcoa, said the closing was undertaken "with great regret," according to the *New York Times*. "The economics are the economics."

Retired journalist Paul Hess told the author that the closing was a gut punch to the community as well as to the mob. "It destroyed the whole downtown. It closed everything down. The economy of New Kensington began to collapse. It was an earthquake."

The Mafia was not spared by the company's decision to abandon the city. Alcoa's closing cut the amount of money Kelly Mannarino made because his organization raked in a substantial number of bets from workers. Employees trolled the shop floor taking bets from other workers that were dropped off at noon each day at a nearby luncheonette near the main gate.

Gambling had created an underground economy in the city that was putting Mannarino's people out of work. Men were hired to work as slot machine repairmen and truck drivers to deliver the pinball and one-armed bandits to clubs and bars. Collectors opened the machines' coin boxes several times a week. Others manned the horse rooms, gambling casinos and numbers drops. Less gambling meant less commissions for bookies, who were paid a percentage based on the amount of bets they received.

For Alcoa, it meant the company would no longer have to deal with the wholesale theft of cutlery and kitchen utensils from their Wear-Ever warehouse, which had "accumulated to an alarming degree," according to a report compiled by the Pittsburgh FBI field office in 1961. Company officials discovered that a salesman who was a friend of Kelly Mannarino was stealing cooking utensils made by Alcoa and fencing the items.

Mannarino didn't provide unemployment compensation to his employees, so men who knew nothing but the gambling trade had no other employment skills to fall back on. Mannarino had no sympathy for the "flunkies" who worked for him reported the FBI in 1972.

The company slowly moved its production facilities to Tennessee, New York, Ohio, California, Illinois, Texas and Iowa. The Vietnam War kept Alcoa from closing completely in 1965. Nevertheless, Alcoa faced competition in the market for its product while the Mannarino organization faced pressure from the FBI and IRS and public-spirited citizens who wanted Kelly Mannarino run out of town.

At the same time Alcoa was pulling up stakes, American St. Gobain, a European glassmaker in the neighboring city of Arnold, announced it was ceasing its manufacturing operations because of competition from cheaper foreign imports. The shutdown of the area's two largest employers put 1,500 out of work, leaving New Kensington with a 10 percent unemployment rate in the early 1970s.

The late Sister Lois Sculco, a professor at Seton Hill University and daughter of the late judge Alexander Sculco, was a New Kensington native and remembered when Alcoa left town. "When Alcoa closed…

what I saw…was a lot of poverty and unemployment. The downtown, like lots of downtown small towns [was] basically gone," she told *Pennsylvania Folklife.*

The prosperous era for Aluminum City and for the mob was over.

17

END OF DAYS

S am Mannarino spent the last years of his life sitting at home in front of his television, snorting cocaine and drinking to the point of intoxication, noted the FBI in its surveillance reports. By the late 1960s, he was no longer active in the mob because his brother had sidelined him and shut off Sam's access to gambling revenue because of his harebrained and money-losing business schemes. Kelly once told an FBI informant that he was thinking about having his brother killed because he had grown tired of his brother's "crazy schemes" and considered putting "out a contract on his brother" because he suspected Sam was slowly sinking into senility and "would be better off…dead," according to a 1962 report.

Special Agent Thomas Forsyth III noted in a 1959 report that Sam was not as "quick-witted, decisive, and sharp as he used to be" and "walks in shuffling fashion with his head down."

Sam suffered a minor stroke and then had a heart attack. Cancer was eating away at his lower abdomen, according to the FBI based on reports from informants. His physician ordered him to stop his "orgiastic" eating and drinking. Mannarino was being treated with radiation and cobalt, and he used cocaine to ease the pain. His good days were spent tending to his legitimate businesses, gas and oil wells, the scrapyard, a grave marker business and his restaurant.

His Ken Iron and Steel Company lost major contracts with Allegheny Ludlum Steel, Alcoa and Union Spring because the companies no longer wanted to be associated with a mobster. Business at his restaurant wasn't doing any better because of his reputation. He spent Saturdays at his restaurant. On Sundays, he stayed home. Mannarino told FBI special agent Thomas Forsyth III that he "stepped down" from the Mafia because he was too sick and too old to continue, but the truth was his brother Kelly had "retired" him because he had attracted unwanted publicity—much to the chagrin of his brother and Pittsburgh's John LaRocca.

Sam thought he had hit it rich when the New Kensington Redevelopment Authority condemned two parcels of land that he owned and used for his scrapyard and a foundry. Assessors valued the property at $350,000, but the authority appealed the award as excessive, and the amount was reduced to $125,000 by the time appeals and court hearings were completed.

Sam first underwent surgery for colon cancer in 1958. He underwent emergency surgery in 1966 after suffering severe stomach pain. His physician, Dr. James. McClowry, noted that the surgeon did not include the reason for the operation in his report. McClowry surreptitiously obtained the test results of the biopsy and gave them to the FBI. Sam Mannarino was dying.

He was admitted to Citizens General Hospital in May 1967 but returned home later in the month so he could die at home. On June 5, his physician advised his family that the cancer was so far advanced that Mannarino would not survive the day and he died that afternoon. Mobsters from California, Chicago, New York and Philadelphia arrived for the funeral. There were so many flowers that the floral arrangements filled two rooms and the hallways of the funeral home. After a priest celebrated a funeral mass, a thirty-eight-car procession followed the hearse to the cemetery.

Sam Mannarino's dream of seeing the Mafia return to power in Cuba was just that, a dream. When Castro entered Havana in January 1959, joyous Cubans ransacked the casinos and destroyed gambling equipment with sledgehammers. The "Las Vegas of the Caribbean" lost up to $2 million a night because of the rampage. Castro shut down the casinos and hotels, which put two thousand Cuban dealers, croupiers, cashiers, musicians, bartenders, waiters and entertainers out of work. With so many Havana residents unemployed and the Havana economy at stake, Castro was forced to reopen the Hilton, Nacional, Riviera, Capri, Comodoro, Tropicana, Saint Johns, Montemarte and Sans Souci under strict government control. The exotic lure of Havana nightlife faded as tourist cash began flowing to Las Vegas and unemployed Americans who worked in the casinos as floor managers and pit bosses returned to the United States to work.

By the late 1960s, New Kensington was on life support. Kelly Mannarino told an FBI agent in 1969 that the once prosperous city was a "dead town."

The city's population peaked at twenty-five thousand between 1920 and 1950, according to census figures, but declined to thirteen thousand by 1971.

Legalized gambling didn't help. Pennsylvania introduced the Daily Lottery in 1972, allowing bettors to play the numbers without fear of arrest. Numbers betting, which averaged $15,000 a day in the late 1950s, had decreased to $4,000 a day by 1968. However, legalization of gambling didn't completely stop sports betting. In 1989, the FBI arrested twenty-three individuals as part of a sports betting operation in the New Kensington area that generated $1 million a month.

Agents reported seeing less and less of Kelly Mannarino in New Kensington because he was spending more time at his winter home in Surfside, Florida, where he was a frequent patron at the Gold Coast Restaurant and Lounge owned by his friend, Joe Sonken.

The *New Kensington Daily Dispatch* kept up its relentless coverage of the Mannarino organization, publishing stories about its gambling haunts, legal troubles and business dealings. The paper's publisher, Eugene Simon, accused the city and Westmoreland County government of being in cahoots with the Mannarino organization. Simon published an editorial listing the number of the Pittsburgh FBI office, urging residents to provide the bureau with any information they had about the Mannarinos.

Simon and Volunteers for Good Government, a coalition of professional and business leaders, organized to break the Mafia's grip on city government and successfully backed the 1961 election of Councilman Edward Zaleski to replace Mayor Ray Gardlock. Simon published the group's manifesto, aimed at removing corrupt leaders like Gardlock.

"With the help of the people, we shall remove the brand of a racket run city. Curbing vice will be placed in the hands of elected officials whose every desire is honesty, morality and proper government, not government by submission to others," read a *Daily Dispatch* editorial.

Gardlock lost his bid for another term as mayor in 1961 and ordered police to raid Mannarino-run bingo games, clubs and bookie joints. "I'm tired of being introduced as the mayor of New Kensington, the hottest town in western Pennsylvania," Garlock complained, reported the *Pittsburgh Press*. "I'm going to cool it as long as I am in office. I'm not a reformer but some of the racket boys have got out of bounds lately."

"I didn't put $25,000 into his campaign to get him elected to have him tell me what to do," Kelly Mannaraino fumed, according to an FBI report. Gardlock informed the Mannarinos that since he was no longer mayor, they should compensate him for the $15,000 in payoffs that he was losing.

They refused, so Gardlock ordered police to start raiding Mannarino gambling joints.

Gardlock wanted to become a state assessor, a job that paid $15,000 annually, but neither former governor George Leader nor governor David Lawrence would hire him because it "would bring a storm of protest from various news media, civic groups and religious organizations," wrote Special Agent Thomas Forsyth III in 1960.

Kelly Mannarino was indicted in 1968 along with John LaRocca and mob bosses in New York and Michigan in connection to kickbacks on a loan from the Teamster Pension Fund. Mannarino was acquitted. In January 1980, Mannarino and Sonny Ciancutti appeared before a federal grand jury in Pittsburgh investigating $150,000 in fraudulent loans involving a $10,000 kickback to a Pittsburgh-area bank loan officer who approved loans to five individuals so they could pay off their gambling debts. As he left the grand jury room, Mannarino's attorney told him he was entitled to a $37.37 appearance fee. "Give it to charity then I can write it off on my income tax," reported the *Pittsburgh Post-Gazette*.

By June, Kelly Mannarino was dead of colon cancer. The crowd at the funeral mass at Mount St. Peter's Church spilled outside the church. Onlookers, reporters and photographers watched as his coffin was carried out of the church.

Mount Saint Peter's Church in New Kensington. Mobsters were baptized, married and buried from the church. *Wikipedia*.

Illness and old age began to catch up with the Mafia. John LaRocca died in 1984. His successor, Mike Genovese, died in 2015. Charles "Chucky" Porter replaced Genovese until Porter went to prison in 1990. Sonny Ciancutti was the last boss of the Pittsburgh mob and was believed to be the last "made" member taking over control over the remnants of the Pittsburgh Mafia. Ciancutti's name surfaced in 1985 during a cocaine investigation involving one of his cousins. In 1992, he was suspected of extorting money from bingo operators in Pennsylvania and Ohio but never charged.

His last arrest was in 2000, along with fifteen others, in a multimillion-dollar gambling network that stretched across Allegheny, Westmoreland and Fayette Counties in southwestern Pennsylvania. The ring generated $500,000 a week during the NFL football season and $300,000 during basketball season. Ciancutti, according to the Pennsylvania State Attorney General's Office, which shut the network down, received 10 percent of the gross. He pleaded guilty to gambling charges and was sentenced to three months of home confinement and twenty months' probation. He died in 2021 at the age of ninety-one.

New Kensington spent decades trying to live down the city's reputation as a "mob town." James Cooper, director of the New Kensington Redevelopment Authority, complained in 1965 about news coverage of the city by Pittsburgh newspapers. "For a number of years, the racket influence has been broken," he told the *Pittsburgh Post-Gazette*. A former mayor told the *Pittsburgh Press* in 1991 that it's been difficult to shake the past. "We are continually subjected to a condition that existed here 30 to 40 years ago and no longer exists but that image won't diminish."

New Kensington has tried to outlive its image as a crime-ridden city, but in the mid-1980s, FBI agents arrested members of the Pagans, Outlaws and Hells Angels motorcycle gangs in New Kensington for selling drugs and illegal weapons. The city also had problems with prostitution and drug use in 2002 after state health officials reported an outbreak of syphilis. Now the city and adjacent towns are plagued with murders, shootings and drug crimes, including the slaying of a police officer.

Meanwhile, local and state political leaders have attempted to attract manufacturing jobs to a city that saw the last vestiges of the Mafia vanish along with its industrial heritage. The State of Pennsylvania awarded $81 million in grants and loans in 2023 to create three hudnred jobs at the New Kensington Advanced Manufacturing Park on the site where Alcoa once stood.

Retired journalist Paul Hess fondly remembered his days covering New Kensington and the mob. He remembered the racketeers he knew and others he kept his distance from. "We covered the stories we knew about. We wrote about what we could see from the outside. We knew very little of what was going on behind the scenes. There was so much excitement. So much fun. I never had so much fun as a reporter in the 1950s."

BIBLIOGRAPHY

Newspapers

Brockville Record and Times (Ontario, CAN)
Chicago Daily Tribune
Chicago Sunday Sun-Times
Chicago Sun-Times
Connellsville Daily Courier
Las Vegas Revue Journal
Latrobe Bulletin
Miami Herald
Miami New Times
Mon Valley Independent
Monessen Daily Independent
Morgantown (WV) Dominion News
New Kensington Daily Dispatch
New York Times
Pittsburgh Gazette Times
Pittsburgh Post
Pittsburgh Post-Gazette
Pittsburgh Press
Pittsburgh Sun-Telegraph
Sarasota News
Wheeling Intelligencer

Wheeling News Register
Winnipeg Tribune
Youngstown Vindicator

Books

Charbonneau, Jean-Pierre. *The Canadian Connection*. Ottawa: Optimum Publishing Company Limited, 1976.

English, T.J. *Havana Nocturne. How the Mob Owned Cuba…and Then Lost It to the Revolution*. New York: Harper Collins, 2007.

Fusco, Nicola, *The Story of Saint Peters Church in New Kensington, Pa*. Pittsburgh: St. Joseph Protectory, 1944.

Guido, George. *Neighborhoods of the Alle-Kiski Valley*. Tarentum, PA: Word Association Publishers, 2021.

Lacy, Robert. *Little Man: Meyer Lansky and the Gangster Life*. New York: Little, Brown, 1991.

Marsili, Dennis. *Little Chicago*. Indiana: Indiana University of Pennsylvania Press, 2015.

May, Allan R. *Welcome to the Jungle Inn: The Story of the Mafia's Most Infamous Gambling Den*. Cleveland, OH: ConAllan Press, 2011.

Moruzzi, Peter. *Havana Before Castro: When Cuba Was a Tropical Playground*. Lawton, UT: Gibbs Smith, 2008.

Rabinovitch, David. *Jukebox Empire: The Mob and the Dark Side of the American Dream*. Lanham, MD: Rowman & Littlefield, 2023.

Skrabec, Quentin. *Aluminum in America*: *A History*. Jefferson, NC: McFarland, 2017.

Smith, George David. *From Monopoly to Competition*: *The Transformation of Alcoa, 1888–1986*. New York: Cambridge University Press, 1988.

Vivian, Cassandra. *Monessen: A Typical Steel Town*. Charleston, SC: Arcadia Publishing, 2002.

Journal Articles

Alcoa New Kensington American Engineering Record, National Parks Service, Department of the Interior, Washington, D.C. March 27, 1998.

King, Rufus. "The Rise and Decline of Coin-Machine Gambling." *Journal of Crime and Criminology* 55, no. 2 (Summer 1964): 199–207.

Magoc, Chris J. "Final Summary Report. Ethnographic Survey of the Following Communities in the Allegheny-Kiskiminetas River Valley: New Kensington Arnold Braeburn Tarentum Brackenridge Natrona West Natrona ('Ducktown') Natrona Heights with Brief Forays into: Vandergrift Buffalo Township." Steel Industry Heritage Corporation, October 25, 1993.

Marshall, Jonathan. "The Dictator and the Mafia: How Rafael Trujillo Participated U.S Criminals to Extend His Power." *Journal of Global Studies* 35, no. 1 (2018).

Mazak-Kahne, Jeanine. "Small-Town Mafia: Organized Crime in New Kensington, Pennsylvania." *Pennsylvania History: A Journal of Mid-Atlantic Studies* 78, no. 4 (October 2011): 355–92.

Meyerhuber, Carl Jr. "The Alle-Kiski Coal Wars, 1913–1919." *Western Pennsylvania Historical Magazine* 63, no. 3 (July 1980): 197–214.

———. "Black Valley: Pennsylvania's Alle-Kiski Valley and the Great Steel Strike of 1919." *Western Pennsylvania History* 62, no. 3 (July 1979): 251–65.

———. "Organizing Alcoa: The Aluminum Workers Union in Pennsylvania's Allegheny Valley, 1900–1971." *Pennsylvania History: A Journal of Mid-Atlantic Studies* 48, no. 3 (July 1981): 195–219.

Mueseler, Christine M. "Alcoa, New Kensington: 'It Was More than a Job… It Was a Way of Life." *Pennsylvania Folklife* 45, no. 2 (Winter 1995–96).

Worral, Simon. "When the Mob Owned Cuba." *Smithsonian*, July 2016.

Dissertations

Mazak-Kahne, Jeanine. "Birthplace of Aluminum, Cradle of Crime: Sphere of Influence in the Deindustrialization of New Kensington, Pennsylvania." PhD diss., Michigan State University, 2009.

Government Documents

Alcoa and the Aluminum Industry in Southwestern Pennsylvania, 1888–1971, National Register of Historic Places, National Park Service, U.S. Department of the Interior, March 11, 1998.

Committee to Study Governmental Operations with Respect to Intelligence Activities, no. 94–755, 94th Congress, 2nd Session.

Doerner, Special Agent Fred W., Jr. "Crime Conditions Miami Beach, Florida." November 15, 1963.

Douce, Special Agent Richard Gordon. "Gabriel Mannarino, Gabriel Ruggiero, Gabriele Rugiero." April 14, 1958.

———. "Samuel Mannarino, Gabriel Mannarino." June 5, 1958.

———. "Stuart Sutor et al." June 19, 1959.

Farrin, Special Agent Samuel. "Revolutionary Directorate." June 8, 1959.

FBI Interview of Hans G. Milton by Special Agent George E. Davis Jr., September 22, 1959.

FBI Interview of Mother Superior Pauline Simons, November 20, 1958.

Forsyth, Special Agent Thomas, III. Samuel Mannarino. October 10, 1966.

Gleichauf, Justin, to Chief, CIA Contact Division Support. "Memorandum of Visit." February 8, 1961.

Interview of Louis Pessolano by Special Agents Richard Gordon Douce and Thomas Forsyth III, January 15, 1959.

Interview of Norman Rothman by FBI, June 26, 1961.

Johnson, Leland L. *U.S. Business Interests in Cuba and the Rise of Castro*. Santa Monica, CA: Rand Corp., 1964.

Mannarino, Joseph "Jo Jo." Interview by Special Agent Richard Gordon Douce, June 5, 1958.

Mannarino, Samuel. Interview by Special Agents William B. Anderson Jr. and Thomas G. Forsyth III, April 14, 1964.

Muller, Edward K., Historic American Buildings Survey Historic America Engineering Record, Westmoreland County, Pennsylvania, National Parks Service, 1994.

National Park Service. *Cold War in South Florida: History Resource Study*. 2004. https://www.nps.gov/parkhistory/online_books/coldwar/florida.pdf.

New Kensington Downtown Historic District, National Parks Service, U.S. Department of the Interior, June 26, 1998.

Pennsylvania Crime Commission. *A Decade of Organized Crime: Report on Organized Crime*. Pittsburgh: Commonwealth of Pennsylvania, 1980.

———. *The Shipment of Gambling Paraphernalia into Pennsylvania and Its Distribution and Sale Within the Commonwealth*. Pittsburgh: Commonwealth of Pennsylvania, 1977.

Report of House Select Committee on Assassinations, 95th Congress, 2nd sess. Washington, D.C. March 29, 1979.

Report of Special Agent Harold Weida. "Theft of 317 Weapons, 16 Blankets, Carbine Rack from Ohio National Guard Armory, Canton, Ohio, Oct. 14, 1958, Stuart Sutor." November 28, 1958.

Report of Special Agent Norman Thompson. "Gabriel Mannarino." February 17, 1958.

Staff Report of the Evolution and Implications of CIA Sponsored Conspiracies Against Castro, House Select Committee on Assassinations, April 16, 1978.

Stone, Hazel. Interview by Special Agents John Flanigan and Franklin Wright, April 18, 1958.

To Chief, Domestic Collection Division, from Jackson Horton, March 11, 1974.

To Director, FBI, from SAC Pittsburgh, August 23, 1961. "Joseph Raymond Merola. Former Criminal Informant of Miami Division."

"Unknown Subjects Alleged Attempt on the Life of Joseph Merola." FBI report, Miami field office, April 8, 1963.

Westmoreland County Recorder of Deeds, Deed Book 614.

Court Cases

Commonwealth v. Truitt, Supreme Court of Pennsylvania, 369 Pa.72 (Pa. 1951), December 19, 1951.

Pessolano v. State, District Court of Appeals, Third District, 166 So. Second 706, August 26, 1964.

Rock-Ola Mfg. Corp. v. Filben Mfg Co., 168 F 2nd 8th Circuit Court of Appeals, August 16, 1948.

Rothman v. United States of America, No. 74-1240, U.S. Court of Appeals, Third Circuit, January 31, 1975.

United States of America v. Norman Rothman, Victor Carlucci, Daniel Hanna, Joseph Merola, Joseph Giordano, Stuart Sutor, 324 F.2nd 620 (Third Circuit, 1963), October 18, 1963.

United States of America v. Victor Carlucci, Joseph Giordano, Daniel Hanna, Norman Rothman, Sturt Sutor, 13136–13141, Court of Appeals, Third Circuit, March 2, 1961.

United States of America v. William W. Rabin, U.S. Court of Appeals for the Seventh District, No. 13804.

United States of America v. William W. Rabin, U.S. District Court for the Northern District of Illinois, No. 60 CSR 348.

Victor Carlucci, Joseph Giordano, Daniel Hanna, Joseph Merola, Norman Rothman and Stuart Sutor v. United States of America, Petition for Writ of Certiorari, U.S. Court of Appeals for the Third Circuit, no. 930, October Term, 1960.

Newspaper Articles

Aikens, Tom, and Richard Gazarik. "New Kensington Was Known as 'Little Las Vegas." *Greensburg Tribune-Review*, n.d.

Buchanan, James. "Miami the Casablanca of the Caribbean." *Miami Herald*, July 20, 1959.

Chicago Daily Tribune. "How Mystery Man Goofed the Perfect Crime." July 4, 1959.

Connellsville Daily Courier. "Ministers Should Tend to Spiritual Duties—Prosecutor." November 8, 1951.

Dolan, Thomas J. "Hazy Portrait of Illinois' Top Stoolie." *Chicago Sunday Sun Times*, December 19, 1976.

Goodfriend, Arthur. "Dust to Dawn in Havana." *New York Times*, November 20, 1951.

Havemann, Ernest. "Unhappy Cuba's Cockeyed Week." *Life* magazine, March 10, 1958.

Hayes, Liz. "Newspaper Weathered Changes Since 1891 but Never Wavered in Commitment to W. Pa." *Tribune-Review*, December 5, 2016.

Hodiak, Bodiak. "Man Seized in Armored Van Theft." *Pittsburgh Post-Gazette*, December 27, 1979.

Huysman, Fritz. "2 Area Men Lose Appeal in Gun Smuggling Case." *Pittsburgh Post-Gazette*, December 2, 1977.

Ireton, Gabriel. "Area $500,000 Armored Van Theft Probed." *Pittsburgh Post-Gazette*, March 7, 1979.

Januzzi, Gene. "District Racket Drive Opened at Mass Meeting." *Pittsburgh Post-Gazette*, January 29, 1951.

Johnsey, Arthur. "Miami Tourist Nabbed with Canadian Loot." *Miami Herald*, March 3, 1959.

Johnson, Stan. "Miami's Businessmen Take to the Air." *Miami Herald*, April 5, 1959.

Johnson, Vince. "Gaming Tax Evasion Trial Finds Four Guilty." *Pittsburgh Post-Gazette*, March 2, 1963.

———. "JFK Frees Gunrunning Who Was Convicted Here." *Pittsburgh Post-Gazette*, January 8, 1963.

———. "New Kensington Cops Tell of Ban on Raids." *Pittsburgh Post-Gazette*, February 26, 1963.

———. "T-Man Spotted, Followed from Gambling House." *Pittsburgh Post-Gazette*, February 21, 1963.

Larsen, Peter, "How Mobster's Son Dr. Cappy Rothman Became a Fertility Pioneer." *Los Angeles Daily News*, September 9, 2023.

Mauro, John T. "New Kensington Pastors Out to Close Raided Club." *Pittsburgh Post-Gazette*, February 25, 1952.

McCarthy, James. "FBI Ace Tells of Wiretap in Vote Fraud." *Pittsburgh Sun-Telegraph*, January 14, 1955.

McCloskey, William. "1959 Gun-Run Case Mystery Deepens." *Pittsburgh Post-Gazette*, February 17, 1977.

Monessen Daily Independent. "Dent and Howes in Agreement." November 8, 1951.

———. "Rehoboth Church Pastor Blames Politics in Move to Oust Him." January 14, 1957.

Morgantown Dominion News. "Arms for Cuban Rebels Apprehended in Plane Here." November 5, 1958.

———. "Firearms Mystery Solved." August 22, 1962.

New Kensington Daily Dispatch. "Federal Agents Smash Nu Ken Gambling, Horse Room Casino." August 25, 1961.

———. "Mannarino Las Vegas Link Cited." April 7, 1962.

———. "The Mannarino Rule." August 29, 1961.

———. "Speedo Faces Grand Jury." September 1, 1959.

———. "Two Beating Victims Won't Press Charges." May 22, 1961.

———. "Two Shot in District; Racket War Blamed." January 7, 1962.

Pittsburgh Gazette Times. "New Kensington Celebrates 25 Years." June 4, 1916.

Pittsburgh Post. Legal Notice, Name Change, Attorney Sidney L. Frankenstein, Giacinto and Domenica Politano Rugiero to George and Domenica Mannarino. February 26, 1925.

Pittsburgh Post-Gazette. "Canada Gives Heave-Ho to Sam Mannarino." October 14, 1966.

———. "Dent Blames Pulpit for Defeat." November 8, 1951.

———. "700 Pastors Start Crime Crusade." January 22, 1951.

———. "2 Judges Name in '59 Gun-Run Case." February 16, 1977.

———. "U.S. to Fight 2 Gun Runners." April 19, 1977.

———. "Winking at the Rackets." January 28, 1953.

Pittsburgh Press. "Fantastic Jewel Thief Hunted from Police 'Brain Center' Here." December 26, 1954.

———. "700 Pastors Open War on Vice, Rackets." January 22, 1951.

Pittsburgh Sun-Telegraph. "Crusader Threatened Over Phone." July 17, 1952.

———. "Direct Evidence Lacking, Defense Argues in Gun Trial." February 3, 1960.

Rodgers, James. "Gun-Gunner Upset by Convict Tag." *Pittsburgh Press*, January 8, 1963.

Sarasota News. "Gun Runner Captured Near Ocala." November 26, 1958.

Schendel, Gordon. "Something's Rotten in the State of Pennsylvania." *Collier's*, November 11, 1950.

Schnier, Samuel. "Where Do Smugglers Get Their Guns?" *Miami Herald*, September 5, 1959.

Sprigle, Ray. "Even the Judge Couldn't Bring Dent Those Votes." *Pittsburgh Post-Gazette*, February 21, 1952.

———. "Homestead 207 Club Glad to Pick Up the (Pay) Check." *Pittsburgh Post-Gazette*, November 29, 1950.

———. "Judges, DA Won't Close the Rackets—Ministers Do." *Pittsburgh Post-Gazette*, February 29, 1952.

———. "Mayor's Choice for New Kensington Police Chief Has Indestructible Cop Title." *Pittsburgh Post-Gazette*, July 3, 1952.

———. "Ministers See Fine on Police Quiz." *Pittsburgh Post-Gazette*, January 23, 1953.

———. "New Kensington Mayor, Along with Monessen Mayor, Connected to Brothels' World." *Pittsburgh Post-Gazette*, July 1, 1952.

———. "Pastors Launch War on Vicious Political Gang." *Pittsburgh Post-Gazette*, February 18, 1952.

———. "Woman Crusader Westmoreland Sheriff Candidate." *Pittsburgh Post-Gazette*, May 13, 1953.

———. "You Don't Buck the Rackets and Keep Your Job." *Pittsburgh Post-Gazette*, February 19, 1952.

Wall Street Journal. "Wastelands. America's Forgotten Nuclear Legacy." October 29, 2013.

Wheeling Intelligencer. "Senate Probers Subpoena 2 Wheeling Downs Officials." July 21, 1958.

Yerace, Tom. "Friends, Employers Praise Former VND Publisher for Journalistic Integrity." *Tribune-Review*, (Greensburg, PA), May 10, 2012.

Interviews

Blakey, G. Robert. Interview by Bill Rockwood. Frontline, https://www.pbs.org.

Hess, Paul. Interviews with the author, September 25 and 26, 2023.

ABOUT THE AUTHOR

Richard Gazarik lives in western Pennsylvania. A former journalist, he has written about organized crime, outlaw motorcycle gangs, drug gangs and corporate corruption. This is his seventh book.

Visit us at
www.historypress.com